Smiles Are Everywhere

The role of humour, laughter and play in healthcare and wellbeing is a hot topic. *Smiles Are Everywhere: Integrating Clown-Play into daily healthcare practice* is a practical handbook aimed primarily at healthcare professionals and those working in healthcare settings who wish to bring play and humour into their work.

Drawing together the authors' considerable experience in practice, research and training in the use of humour in healthcare settings, this book works to bring theory into practice in a simple, user-friendly manner. Central to *Smiles Are Everywhere* is the understanding that healthcare professionals are striving to deliver patient-centred care and that the activities suggested can be integrated into existing methods of care delivery. The book includes:

- A rationale for why and where laughter and play are beneficial in healthcare settings
- Guidelines for integrating Clown-Plays into your own practice
- Advice on strategies and approaches
- More than 50 clearly laid out activities and ideas developed and adapted by the authors.

Ideal for healthcare professionals as well as anyone working in a healthcare setting, the ideas presented here can also be translated to educational, corporate and training environments.

Bernie Warren is an internationally respected researcher, teacher and writer on the role of the arts in healthcare and education. In 2001 he created *Fools For Health,* which runs Clown-Doctor programs for all ages and for more than 10 years worked in hospitals and healthcare facilities as 'Dr Haven't-a-Clue'.

Peter Spitzer is the Medical Director, co-founder and Inaugural Chairman of the Humour Foundation charity dedicated to promoting the health benefits of humour. He delights in teaching humour techniques to healthcare undergraduates and postgraduates as well as the education and corporate sectors.

Smiles Are Everywhere

Integrating Clown-Play into healthcare practice

Bernie Warren and Peter Spitzer

Routledge
Taylor & Francis Group
LONDON AND NEW YORK

First published 2014
by Routledge
4 Park Square, Milton Park, Abingdon, Oxon OX14 4RN
605 Third Avenue, New York, NY 10017

Routledge is an imprint of the Taylor & Francis Group, an informa business

British Library Cataloguing in Publication Data
A catalogue record for this book is available from the British Library

Library of Congress Cataloging in Publication Data
Warren, Bernie, 1953–
Smiles are everywhere : integrating clown-play into healthcare practice / Bernie Warren and Peter Spitzer.
pages cm
Includes bibliographical references and index.
1. Wit and humor–Therapeutic use. 2. Wit and humor in medicine.
3. Clowns. 4. Psychotherapy. I. Spitzer, Peter (Peter G.) II. Title.
RC489.H85W37 2013
616.89′1653–dc23 2013003437

ISBN: 978–0–415–50514–7 (hbk)
ISBN: 978–0–415–50515–4 (pbk)
ISBN: 978–0–203–76868–6 (ebk)

Typeset in Times New Roman
by Swales & Willis, Ltd, Exeter, Devon

Contents

Illustrations

Preface

Take two clowns, and call me in the morning – or why should I listen to you?

Bernie: As the first-born son in a Jewish medical family I was expected to follow in my grandfather's footsteps and become a Physician. Needless to say, I did not follow the path chosen for me by my family. Nevertheless all my life I have always been involved in some aspect of healing and / or health promotion. Much of my professional work has been concerned with the use of drama with people who, by illness, accident of birth, or social circumstances have in some way been disempowered or disenfranchised, I wanted to help them in some way to overcome their individual challenges. In addition to my work in the arts and community, since my early teens I have been a student and practitioner of Qigong (Chinese breathing exercises for health and energy), which is one of the three pillars of traditional Chinese Medicine. Currently I run regular Qigong classes with cancer patients, heart and stroke patients, seniors and normal neurotics.

I grew up in a household where dinner conversation often focused on medical topics, remember we were Jewish and our family has its fair share of neurotics and hypochondriacs. My Poppa (my mother's father) was a doctor. He qualified in 1922 and practised medicine until his death in 1966. He was a modest man, never sought glory or the 'limelight' but 'notable' and learned doctors (including the Queen's personal physician) often sought his advice on a variety of medical matters. He lived his life by the proverb, 'a cheerful heart does good like a medicine' and his obituary stressed that he had 'a good bedside manner and a fine sense of humour'. He used humour as part of his act. For him it came naturally, he had a gift and he used it to make patients smile or laugh.

My Poppa was not unique. Like so many other 'old time' family doctors he believed that bedside manner was more than half the healing process. Something, many would argue, that modern western technological medicine has forgotten. From my grandfather I learned for myself the value of laughter. As I grew up I began to realise that one of the few skills I have is that I can make people laugh and that humour, most notably physical humour, transcends language. One result of this was that early in the 1980s I started to research the role of humour in healing and healthcare and in particular the work of clowns in hospitals.

My day job since 1992 has been as a full professor in the School of Dramatic Art at the University of Windsor. Since 1999 I have managed to secure several research grants to examine the role of clowns playing in hospitals and healthcare

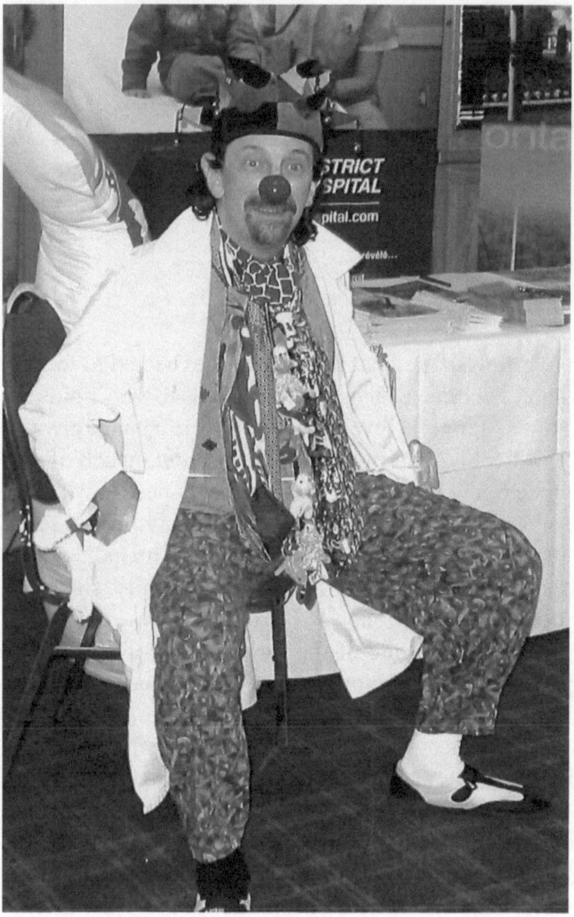

Figure 0.1 Haven't takes a rest

settings. One result of this work was that in 2001, after several years of working on a book on the work of *Le Rire Medecin* in Paris,[1] I founded *Fools For Health*: a Clown-Doctor program based in hospitals in Windsor, Ontario and began my life as Dr Haven't-a-Clue visiting young and old in hospitals. In 2002 I had been in Spain doing research on the role of clowns in hospitals and heard that Peter would be in Paris at the same time and we arranged to meet.

Peter: I was flying airplanes before I had my driver's licence. My first passion was to become a commercial pilot but failing the eyesight test brought these dreams to a halt. I finished high school and applied to study Architecture at University. At the last minute I changed to Medicine. My Jewish mother cried for joy! . . . At last 'my son the Doctor'.

Nevertheless my personality drew me to the arts and during my Medical studies I found time to explore and gain experience in stage, film and modern dance. Not long after graduation as a result of frustration with the medical system I went *Walkabout* and travelled the world for a couple of years. During this time I worked in London and shared a squat with a travelling circus troupe that included JP Bell, a professional Australian performer. He was a clown who wanted to be a doctor and I was a doctor who wanted to be a clown. This meeting sowed the seeds of what would later become *The Humour Foundation.*[2]

On returning to Australia I studied acupuncture, hypnosis, musculo-skeletal techniques, all of which allowed me to take a more holistic approach to patient care as I entered general practice. Humour, magic and Clown-Plays were elements used in my interactions with my patients and my staff. In 1997 I co-founded *The Humour Foundation* and I began my life as Dr Fruit-Loop, a clown-doctor visiting sick kids in hospitals.

Figure 0.2 Bernie, tree, Peter

In 2002 I was awarded a Churchill Fellowship to study the impact of clown-doctor programs on the healthcare systems around the world. As part of this journey I visited *Le Rire Medecin* in Paris. I was exhausted and nearly missed the scheduled appointment with Bernie.

Another fine mess you've gotten me into

We met on a very rainy evening in a cafe in Paris. It was a meeting that very nearly didn't happen. Luckily, despite the weather and our schedules, the meeting did take place.

Our Paris meeting was a significant turning point in both our lives. We started slowly with some professional correspondence and shared research. Slowly but surely we not only became research colleagues but firm friends.

Over the last ten years we have collaborated more and more. We have run workshops and made conference presentations together for healthcare professionals and artists all over the world and over the last couple of years have started to write together. Most recently we co-authored an article for *The Lancet*, 'Laughing to longevity' on the work of Elder-Clowns, professional performers who work with older people living in various residential care facilities, such as nursing homes, long-term care and in dementia units.

Smiles are everywhere – the book . . .the musical comes later

Like most of our work together this book started as an offhand remark! We were discussing the work of LaughterBosses[3] for *The Lancet* article and were intrigued by the possibility of how to inject humour and play into the broader practice of healthcare. As usual this seemingly harmless exploration of ideas got us into another fine mess, yet another mega project to tax our time, energy and household budgets. If you don't believe us, just ask our wives!

Smiles Are Everywhere: Integrating Clown-Play into daily healthcare practice is a practical handbook aimed primarily at healthcare professionals and artists working in healthcare settings who wish to bring play and humour into their work. It draws together our considerable experience in practice, research and training in the use of humour and play in healthcare settings.

Smiles Are Everywhere is not a dry scholarly text, rather it is a research-based practical book that brings theory into practice in a simple user friendly and easy to read manner. Central to this book is the understanding that healthcare professionals are attempting to deliver patient-centred care. In it we present a rationale for why and where laughter and play are beneficial in healthcare settings. Additionally we provide guidelines, as well as simple ideas and activities, to help enable you to transform your own daily practice. Moreover, while generally healthcare delivery *is* a serious business (where procedures and appropriate drug regimens are paramount – the *what* of healthcare), this book looks at the notion of *how* the delivery of healthcare can be enhanced by adding a smile to help deliver evidence-based best practice.

One of the primary concepts behind this book is that you do not need to be a skilled performer to employ activities suggested within it. Rather we provide ideas and activities that can be incorporated into a range of healthcare practices and that build on, and can be integrated into, the skills that you already have.

While the primary focus of this practical handbook is on *healthcare* practice, the concepts, guidelines and activities presented here are also applicable in educational and corporate settings and in continuing professional education and training.

A few words about *Clown-Play*

Throughout this book we use the term *Clown-Play*[4] to describe 'any playful activity or intervention drawn from the work of clowns in healthcare settings' that may also be used to bring play and humour into healthcare and other workplace settings. Clown-plays include such activities as: physical humour, verbal humour, Reminiscence techniques, music and song structures, and, other creative interventions e.g. bedside magic. In the context of this book we are using this term to describe activities consciously employed to inject playfulness, humour/laughter into daily interactions to, among other things, promote healing, improve quality of life, aid communication, or, simply to make your job easier and more enjoyable.

AADS: Acquired Amusement Deficiency Syndrome – It's an epidemic

People who are serious all the time suffer from AADS. This condition poses a threat to quality of life. Most people do not appreciate quality of life until it is taken away, for example by an accident or illness. AADS gradually erodes the capacity to tap into joyfulness of life, so that you do not even realise that you have lost it.

Some of the symptoms of AADS include:

- When the annual report is the preferred bedtime reading
- Prone to making mountains out of mole hills
- Emotional constipation
- Difficulty in swallowing humour
- Persistent soreness about almost everything
- Hardening of the attitude
- Terminal seriousness

AADS is rampant within the cash-strapped, evidence-based, outcomes-driven modern healthcare systems worldwide. The only cure is to inject humour and play into healthcare and the community, and that is what our book intends to do, for as you will see smiles can be found anywhere.

In the next chapter we look at some of the evidence to support the value of humour and play in healthcare.

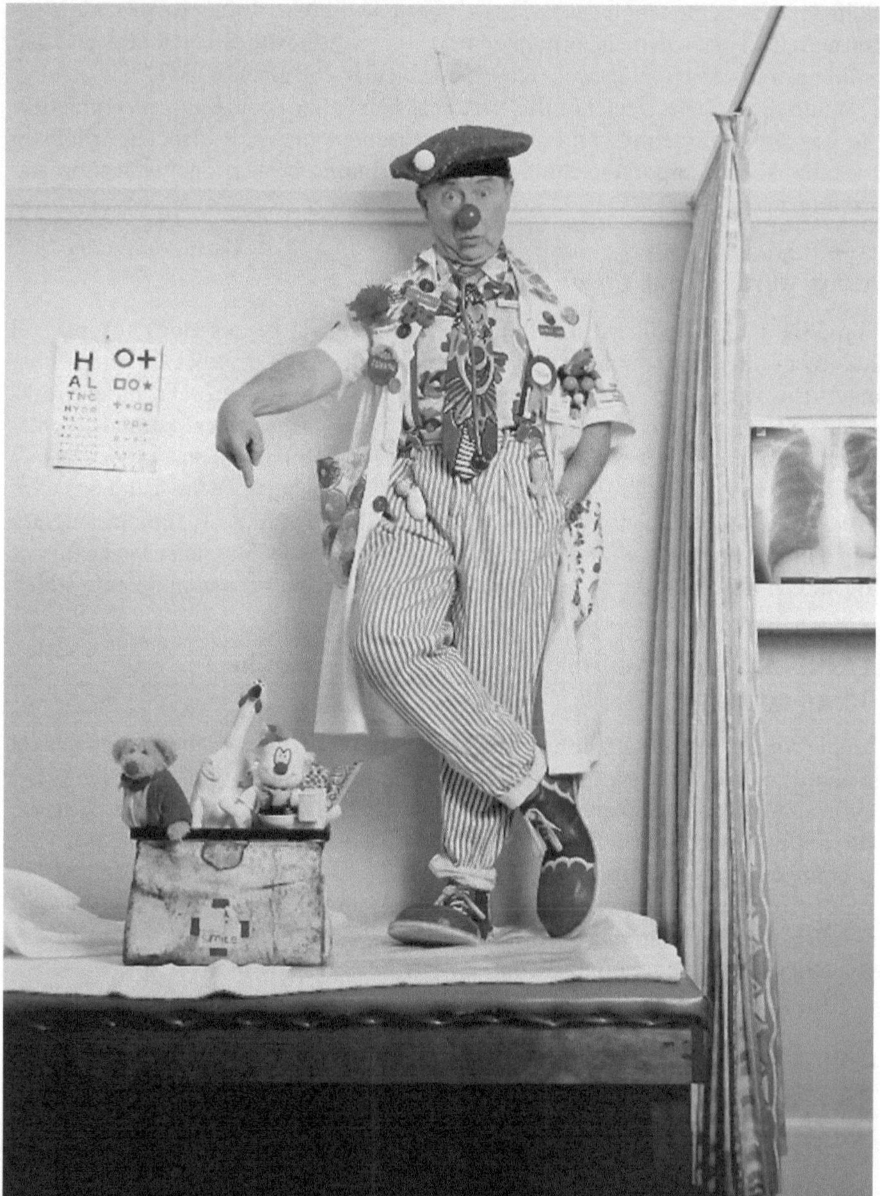

Figure 0.3 Fruit-Loop at work

Notes

1 The work with Caroline Simonds, Directrice of *Le Rire Medecin* – one of the premier Clown-Doctor programs in the world.
2 We were a small group of people who founded the charitable organisation – *The Humour Foundation*.
3 A LaughterBoss is a healthcare professional working with seniors who is further trained in the use of play and humour in their facility.
4 Historically other writers have used other terms (e.g. *Jest*, *Jeu, Lazzi*, *Shtick,* or simply Play) to describe these and/or similar activities.

Acknowledgements

First and foremost we must thank our long-suffering wives, Sheila and Judy, as this book would not have been completed without their patience and support. In particular, I (BW) want to thank Judy Spitzer for putting up with me descending on her house and turning it into a writing 'war room' for 10 days in August 2012! Thank you both for tolerating our Skype calls at all hours of the day and night and with us disappearing for hours at a time to discuss and write this book.

Our editorial assistants, Candace Hind and Amber Milliken, cannot be thanked enough. Candace read many drafts of this book and made several very insightful comments, particularly related to references and content. Amber worked tirelessly to make the final manuscript presentable. She proof-read the final drafts, reformatted them, and re-wrote and formatted the Clown-Plays and the At-a-Glance Grid.

We also want to thank all the artists sharing humour and play in hospitals and healthcare facilities around the world who, directly or indirectly, have stimulated us to pass on skills, techniques, creative ideas to others through this book.

Acknowledgement is due to *Les cahiers de l'idiotie* for permission to reprint material from Bernie Warren's article 'Foolish Medicine: Some connections between modern clown-doctors and medieval fools', which first appeared in *Le Clown: une utopie pour notre temps (Numero 3).*

Finally we wish to thank all the patients, residents, clients and students with whom we have been privileged to work. You have been good teachers for us – we have learned something from each of you.

To all these people (friends, students, colleagues, clients, patients and residents alike) we dedicate this book.

Bernie Warren
Harrow
Ontario, Canada

Peter Spitzer
Bowral
NSW, Australia

1 Why Clown-Play belongs in healthcare

In this section we present a brief overview of the importance of play, not just for children but also for adults. We also will look at: the growing body of research and scholarly writing on the therapeutic value of laughter and play in healthcare; and the work of modern clowns in hospitals and healthcare facilities.

As the primary focus of this book is the practical application of clown-plays within your practice, this review will be limited to major themes and developments that help support this. For those readers interested in a more detailed examination of the literature we do present an expanded list of references in the resources section.

Not just for children: The value of play and games across the lifespan

All mammals play, and the higher the species, the greater the amount of play.[1] Play is an integral part of all human culture wherever it is found and in whatever state of advancement the culture maybe.[2] Many writers[3] have commented about the importance of play and games[4] in the development of cultures and healthy well-adjusted human beings. While writers on play have argued with one another about the meaning and significance of play and games (what, how, where and why we play, who we play with and what this all means to our supposed sanity and social adjustment in an ever changing world), they are almost unanimous in the belief that humans have a long childhood for a reason.

However, children don't read these theories and debates. Children play unconstrained by psychological and sociological theories about why they do so. They play in developed and developing cultures. They play in water and on land. They play in affluent and poor neighbourhoods; in houses and fields; in streets and alleys; and even in bombed-out buildings in war-torn countries. They play with toys, with inanimate objects and with each other. They play because playing and games are fun. If playing isn't fun children stop, and either change the activity or take their ball and go home.

While adults for the most part believe that play is, 'something children do and adults don't'.[5] This really isn't the case. Adults create things. They build and decorate; they play board games and with ideas. They play with words and numbers

Figure 1.1 Two noses are better than one

while doing puzzles and crosswords. They play competitive sports to let off steam and to 'de-stress'.

Play, creativity and adaptability are connected. Our ability to adapt to new environments, protocols and situations are all linked to the ability to play, imagine and improvise. As a species our adaptability and the ability to imagine are essential to courtship and falling in love. To empathise and sympathise, to listen and adapt to our partner's fears, likes, dislikes and needs is becoming increasingly important as part of the mating rituals of the human animal.

Rediscovering the mind of a child is essential to all innovation. For children at play are role models for innovators and agents of change and have much to say to companies about productivity. Young children who ask parents those unanswerable questions (e.g. 'why is the sky blue', 'what does God look like') are the quintessential researchers. They ask difficult questions unencumbered by social constraints. They see *The Emperor's New Clothes* for what they really are! Technology, software development and advertising companies all expect their employees to be able to 'think outside the box'. Corporations and companies place great store on brainstorming and team building both of which are largely based on playfulness and game structures. Moreover innovation, creativity and even lovemaking are all linked with our ability to be playful!

Linking play to smiles and laughter

When a child (or an adult) engages in a playful creative activity they can become lost in a 'creative moment': a liminal state[6] that brings together physical, intellectual, emotional and spiritual aspects of our being in a way that offers unique opportunities for transformation to take place. If one watches children at play, whether they are playing a game (e.g. Tag or Hide and Seek) or are involved in more spontaneous dramatic play (e.g. Cops and Robbers or playing with dolls), they get lost in the moment. That's one of the reasons why children at play often are not conscious of time: as when Mum says, 'Where have you been? Don't you realise what time it is?' However, because children have been lost in their play, itself a liminal state, they frequently **don't** realise what time it is.

Liminal acts must be undertaken in a liminal state. In a rite such as 'fire walking', the thought that fire can burn must be 'cleansed' before the participant in the ritual actually walks through the fire. The participant cannot be thinking about the fire when they are walking over or through it. Remember the feelings you felt the moment just before your first kiss with someone you loved outside of your family. At that instant, you were preparing to be lost in the act of the kiss.

When we laugh all elements of our self (mind, body, emotion, soul) are united in what may be called a 'healing moment', creating the potential for healing to take place. It must be made clear that laughter in and of itself does not cure any disease. However, the laughter may act as a catalyst for internal physiological changes to occur.

Is laughter good medicine? Putting humour and health in perspective

Over the last several decades (fuelled in part by the biblical quote, 'a cheerful heart does good like a medicine') there has been considerable inquiry, both scientific and anecdotal, into the physiological effects and psychological benefits of humour and laughter.[7] Based on this research, there is evidence to suggest that humour and laughter have a positive effect on emotions, physiological processes and pain tolerance.

This research into Gelotology, the effects of humour on the human body, led in 1988 to the formation of an Association for Applied and Therapeutic Humour. They define Therapeutic Humour as 'any intervention that promotes health and wellness by stimulating a playful discovery, expression or appreciation of the absurdity or incongruity of life's situations'. These beliefs, that humour is 'therapeutic' and that laughter is 'good medicine', underpin the premise of this book not only that 'Smiles Are Everywhere,' but also that smiles and laughter are good for you.

Therapeutic humour[8] has been used in a wide range of settings to achieve a variety of outcomes including: improved mood and decreased anxiety,[9] facilitating the psychotherapeutic or treatment process,[10] and reduced stress and increased relaxation,[11]

Laughter affects the mind and the body. There are many reasons why laughter makes us feel good. In the field of psychoneuroimmunology studies have shown that laughter can produce a drop in serum (cortisol) stress hormone; enhance immune system functioning and lead to a reduction of stress hormones in the body,[12] while a recent study found that humour and laughter triggers the brain's reward centres.[13]

The effects of humour and laughter on physical discomfort have also been studied.[14] An examination of the impact of stress on inflammatory disorders, asthma, cancer and heart disease suggests that humour and positive affect can improve prognosis in these situations.[15]

Fry and associates[16] describe the impact of mirth and laughter on respiration and blood pressure. Other recent studies have looked at the effects of psychosocial stress on cardiovascular disease,[17] and on how laughter reduces risks of cardiovascular incidents.[18] These and other studies show that laughter produces beneficial respiratory and cardiovascular effects. Laughter stimulates respiration, relaxes arteries and improves blood flow as well as oxygen saturation of peripheral blood. After a transient rise there is a drop in blood pressure and positive effects on hypertension and diabetes have also been noted.

Other studies have shown that laughter reduces pain and that a relaxation response is experienced after laughter. Research in the field of Positive Psychology[19] has shown positive effects on performance, mood, optimism, anxiety and depression and also that laughter enhances communication and is positively associated with emotional stability.

In the next section we will look at how clowns came to work in healthcare, the many types of clown-plays they employ and some of the research on the benefits of these plays with various healthcare contexts.

Notes

1 Sutton-Smith, 1979.
2 Padmanabhachari quoted by Brewster in Avedon and Sutton-Smith, 1971.
3 E.g. Groos, 1896; Huzinga, 1955; Cohen, 1987; Winnicott, 1971; Callois, 1961; Sutton-Smith, 1979; Brown, 2009 etc.
4 There are several definitions of the distinction between play and games. I have always liked Callois' explanation that:

- PLAY is free, separate, uncertain and unproductive, yet regulated and make-believe, while
- A GAME is a specialised form of play: one that has order and structure – a beginning, middle and an end.

More simply put, *Games* have rules that must be followed, while *Play* has rules that are malleable and/or changeable and unlike games has no predetermined end.
5 Cohen, 1987.
6 Liminal is a word borrowed from social anthropology. It was originally applied to rites of passage. *Limen* in Latin means a margin, threshold, or boundary and a liminal act is where the participant passes over a real threshold such as walking through fire or a socially determined boundary such as puberty.
7 E.g. Bennett, M. and Lengacher, C., 2006a, 2006b, 2008, 2009; Berk et al., 1989; Cousins, 1979; Fry, 1992; Hudak et al., 1991; Martin, 2004; Miller et al., 2006; Rosner, 2002.
8 The Association for Applied and Therapeutic Humor (AATH) defines therapeutic humour, as 'any intervention that promotes health and wellness by stimulating a playful discovery, expression, or appreciation of the absurdity or incongruity of life's situations'. This intervention may enhance health or be used as a complementary treatment. . .to facilitate healing or coping whether physical, emotional, cognitive, social or spiritual.
9 Morgan and Jorm, 2008.
10 Penson et al., 2005; Richman, 1995.
11 Sutorius, 1995.
12 Berk et al., 1989.
13 Mobbs et al., 2003.
14 Hudak et al., 1991; Mahoney, Burroughs and Hieatt, 2001.
15 Hassad, 2001.
16 Fry, 1977; 1992; Fry and Savin, 1988; Fry and Stoft, 1971.
17 O'Keefe et al., 2004.
18 Miller et al., 2006.
19 Gelkopf and Kreitler,1996; Snyder and Lopez, 2006.

2 How clowns play

A brief history of clowns using laughter and play for health[1]

In this section we look at the evolution internationally of clown programs in healthcare. We will examine the plays used by clowns and the research on the effect of these plays on patients and staff. After this we'll look at developing relationships with staff as a means of implementing play and humour within healthcare settings. At the end of this section we will look forward to the next, in which we present ways for staff to work without clowns.

Fools are everywhere[2] – even in hospitals

Fools have been found in almost every human society and have been known by many names including *parasite, clod, sot, buffoon, stultor, jester* and today simply as *clown*. All these 'fools by any other name' used playfulness and humour to make

Figure 2.1 Portrait of clown as a young man

people laugh, to change their mood and to feel better. Like fools throughout history, clowns who work in hospitals are also know by many names, for example *therapeutic clown, hospital clown, medical clown, caring clown* and *clown-doctor* (the term we will use throughout this chapter).

The roots of the work of clown-doctors begin before scientific inquiry, randomised controlled trials and the evidence-based medicine that underpin Gelotology.[3] Modern clown-doctors, if asked to comment on the influences on their work, usually make reference to famous mime teachers (e.g. Lecoq, Decroux, Pochinko, Gaulier), or circus clowns (e.g. Grock, Oleg Popov, Emmett Kelly), or characters made famous by film or television performers (e.g. Jerry Lewis, Lucille Ball, Charlie Chaplin, Rowan Atkinson). However, we believe that the roots of clown-doctors' work goes back much further, to the practices of medieval fools, particularly court jesters, whose jests were employed to change the mood of kings, clergy and the common people.

Clown-doctors and the tradition of fools as healers

Clown-doctors are not medical doctors,[4] they are professional artists specially trained to work in a hospital. Usually clown-doctors work in pairs, wear a red nose, use a minimal amount of stage make-up, wear a white lab coat[5] and are most often referred to as *doctor* (e.g. Dr Haven't-a-Clue). Their work is not mere entertainment. They interact with patients, their families and the healthcare team seeking to promote wellness and to improve quality of life through the use of artistry that includes music, improvisational play, magic and humour. Clown-doctors should be viewed as the latest in a long line of fools who have worked to help heal mind, body and soul, something they have done from at least the time of Hippocrates.

According to research conducted by Cotlove, Hippocrates' hospital[6] on the island of Kos, 'maintained constant troupes of players and clowns in the quadrangle in the belief that mood influenced healing and that convalescents ought to be kept happy and amused'[7]. In the 12th century, Rahere, one of Henry the first's court jesters, founded St Bartholomew's Hospital in London, England.[8] This is perhaps not a surprise as one of the primary functions of the court jester was to help cure the monarch or noble when they were feeling melancholy,[9] and jesters were often sent to help alleviate distress during serious illness e.g. *Il Matello* who had amazing success in helping Alfonso D'Este forget his serious illness.[10] And to this day in several cultures clowns perform healing ceremonies, often as a means of driving out spirits that their culture believes cause disease.[11]

At the very end of the 19th century, *The Fratellini Brothers* (a famous clown trio) started making irregular visits to hospitals. This is usually acknowledged as the starting point for the modern practice of clowns visiting hospitals and other healthcare settings. From 1908 onward regular reports begin of other circus clowns performing occasional clown rounds, predominantly in children's wards.[12]

Modern professional clown-doctors began working in hospitals in 1986 when Michael Christensen (*Dr. Stubbs*), along with Jeff Gordon (*disorderly gordoon*), first set foot in a hospital. Their ground-breaking work led to the first Clown-Doctor program and to the formation of the *Big Apple Circus Clown Care Unit.*[13] While initially this work was confined to paediatric units, increasingly clown-doctors are now working with patients of all ages and in all areas of hospitals.[14] Currently clown-doctors work in more than a dozen countries around the world[15] and see literally tens of thousands of patients every year.

The influence of medieval fools on modern hospital clowning

The *practice* of clown-doctors, how they dress and what they actually do while in a hospital, can be traced back to the costumes and jests[16] employed by medieval fools, particularly jesters at the courts of kings and nobles.

By all accounts medieval fools, much like clown-doctors, practised *empty pockets clowning*. They carried very few props around with them and when they did use objects they were those found in the room. However the one exception was the fool's bauble or sceptre. Several scholars discuss the significance of this object and fools' various ways of interacting with it.[17] Here we simply wish to observe that modern clown-doctors often carry with them their own baubles. Most wear a stethoscope around their neck that, in combination with a red nose, signifies that I am a clown-doctor, in much the same way as a fool's costume and bauble signified who they were.

Clown-doctors also often use finger puppets that they will speak to and personify in much the same way as the jester embodied his bauble with life. Dr Haven't-a-Clue carries with him a toilet plunger. When the rubber plunger is on, it is used to perform 'Belly-Button-Otomies'. More usually he removes the rubber plunger and places a finger puppet on the wooden stick and uses it much the same way as the jester used his bauble.

If scholars such as Welsford and Otto are to be believed the list of skills and jests attributed to medieval fools is almost limitless.[18] This is in large part because 'The number of fools is infinite'.[19] While the number of clowns working in hospitals is not infinite, nevertheless currently there are literally thousands of individuals working as clowns in hospitals. No two clowns are the same. Nevertheless there are many commonalities in the ways that they work.

- *Verbal Jests* e.g. telling jokes, witticisms, speaking nonsense, making up languages and/or making animal sounds, reciting poetry, *verse capping*[20] and delivering news and/or commenting on current events.

Many fools, particularly court jesters, were reputed to be quick witted and quick tongued. They would play with words and sounds and recite poetry, running the gamut from elegiac to the nonsensical. They would also discuss topics and deliver news that no one else could.

Today in hospital many clown-doctors are very verbal. They will talk in gibberish, tell jokes, make puns and even play versions of verse capping e.g. by telling a story one sentence at a time, with each clown adding the next line trying to outdo their partner.

They will discuss the weather or talk about last night's television or sports events or politics. They will use any topic that enables them to form a bridge between them and the patient, their family or the healthcare team. It also helps the patient to stay connected to the outside world, much like a jester bringing news to the medieval court. This is often particularly helpful in the most tense of situations e.g. when working with palliative care patients and their families.

Palliative care work usually involves singing or playing soft lullabies and being quiet, compassionate and respectful. However sometimes, it is also appropriate for the clown-doctors to be loud and to make conversations about topics that are off limits to healthcare professionals,[21, 22] such as politics, sex and religion, but that acknowledge the adult palliative patient as a living breathing human being. For as Patch Adams has often said, no one is ever dying. We are all living until we take our last breath.

- *Physical Jests* e.g. juggling, puppetry; dancing; tumbling and pratfalls.

Many medieval fools were accomplished dancers and jugglers. Their dances would include the formal dances performed at court and impromptu pieces created on the spur of the moment that might involve dancing on, or with, furniture and end with them tumbling or falling comically. As puppeteers they would animate their baubles, many of which had elaborate faces carved on them,[22] and engage in a conversation with them, often at the expense of the assembled company. As jugglers they would juggle objects found in the room e.g. food, cutlery or crockery.

Clown-doctors use a lot of physical business but have certain limits placed on them by space, and by health and safety concerns. Tumbling and pratfalls are therefore limited. However, walking into walls is a fairly common practice e.g. they will often attempt to leave a patient's room via a wall and if space permits perform a backwards roll as a punctuation to the jest.

Clown-doctors dance, a lot. They dance with chairs, with unattached IV poles, with patients, their families, nurses, doctors and with each other. Their dances may be parodies of known dance styles (everything from ballroom through ballet to hip-hop) or they may be completely unique, improvised on the spur of the moment.

Many clown-doctors juggle. Some clowns such as Dr Dan-D-Lion will juggle alone, while others such as Dr Fifi and Dr Ops sometimes juggle objects between each other. Clown-doctors use juggling balls, objects found in the room and some even juggle bedpans, first checking that they are clean!

- *Musical Jests* e.g. singing; playing musical instruments, making music with everyday objects

Fools, especially those at court, were often accomplished singers and musicians. As musicians, they would play the harp or lute or flute, and sometimes even coax music out of everyday objects. They would sing well-known songs of the time and songs of their own making which might range from beautiful ballads to nonsense ditties. They would use these songs to poke fun at the assembled company, to pass comment on current events and to soothe troubled minds.

Today modern clown-doctors use song extensively. They sing familiar songs to change a mood, to help relax or to amuse. Some make up nonsense songs, using animal sounds or nonsense words sung to the tunes of well-known songs. Dr. Cha Cha, Dr. Tilly and others often play a game called 'Stump the Chump' where a patient suggests a word or phrase and the clowns must sing a song that either begins with it or contains it. While others like Dr. Haven't-a-Clue often spontaneously sing a couple of lines from a song that includes a phrase or comment spoken to him by a patient or healthcare worker. Still others like Dr. Bob in France are human jukeboxes with an almost limitless supply of songs. While Dr. Merry Kay!, a trained opera singer, will often sing snippets of arias.

Clown-doctors are also often accomplished musicians. Dr. Giraffe is a very accomplished flautist and Dr. Twinkle-Toes a multi-instrumentalist. Some will play music on surgical instruments, like Dr. Merry Kay! who plays classical melodies on a large syringe! Dr. Cha Cha plays virtuoso heavy metal rock and punk music on her ukulele. Dr. Diddle used to rest her portable electric piano on her 'ample bosom' (her costume had large stiff cones sewn into it), while she played everything from the latest pop tune to a Chopin nocturne on it.

- *Specialty Jests* e.g. performing magic tricks.

Court fools performed a wide variety of magic tricks especially card tricks and prestidigitation. In hospitals today a variety of magical tricks are performed that range from the truly magical to the truly stupid. Often the complexity of the magic reflects the level of expertise, as some clown-doctors are also stage magicians while others have no special training at all. In Australia, Dr. Fruit-Loop performs many up-close magic tricks at the bedside that dazzle and amaze sick children. On the other hand Dr. Haven't-a-Clue can make everyone in the room disappear (by very theatrically closing his eyes) or make himself become invisible (by asking everyone in the room to close their eyes) both of which prove he is a master of 'stupid magic'.

Research on clowns working in healthcare settings

The skills and attributes of fools and jesters, the antecedents of clown-doctors, and their perceived positive effect on the sanity and health of both cultures and individuals have been discussed in detail by several authors.[24]

Over the past several years, there have been many reports about the work of clowns in hospitals (most focusing on the effects of the work with children), and of Clown-Doctor programs around the world.[25] More recently there have been some studies published concerning the perceptions of doctors, nurses, parents and children towards clown-doctors,[26] the effects of clown-doctors on: pre-operative anxiety,[27] in vitro fertilization,[28] and medication use.[29, 30]

Research on work in hospitals (Warren, 2008b) shows that clowns use of humour and play helps:

- *reset the clock* (i.e. reframe perceptions of time) for patients and staff – especially valuable in emergency waiting rooms and for patients waiting for surgery;
- patients and their family take their mind off illness;
- brighten the mood of nurses, doctors and other healthcare staff;
- reduce anxiety in young children awaiting surgery;
- act as a *distraction* during minor bedside procedures:
  - (e.g. inserting an intravenous drip, or a Ventolin treatment);
- extend the range of motion for stroke and aphasia patients;
- encourage patients with a tracheotomy or aphasia to speak;
- reduce the use of pain and anti-depressant medication;
- reduce the overall length of stay in the hospital;
- increase staff morale;
- reduce staff absenteeism;
- increase satisfaction with rehabilitation programs.

The research on clowns' use of humour and play with seniors has just begun and has primarily focused on the effects of the clowns' work on the quality of life and health of seniors.[31] However, the SMILE study, a world-first three-year randomised controlled trial evaluating the effects of humour therapy on residents with dementia in residential care facilities, has just finished. The results from this extensive research show that humour increases staff morale, decreases agitation and reduces the use of atypical anti-psychotics.[32]

This research on work in residential facilities shows that clowns help seniors:

- connect to their immediate surroundings;
- recognise family members;
- remember the past;
- improve cognitive functioning and communication skills;
- increase the quality of life for seniors, their families, and for the healthcare staff who work with them.

Clowns working with staff

In recent years, there has been a move away from the performer acting alone to them working hand in hand with staff to deliver humour and laughter in healthcare. The LaughterBoss initiative, begun by Dr Peter Spitzer in Australia, is an example of this. Peter saw the impact of clown visits at aged care facilities, but also recognised that the clowns were not able to make regular visits, which limited the impact and connection with everyone in the facility. The commonest complaint was, 'Why don't you come more often?' This signalled an inadequately met need. With the increasing demand for clowns to visit aged care facilities, The LaughterBoss (a modern day equivalent of the court jester for aged care) was born.

A LaughterBoss is a healthcare professional who has been trained to introduce and use humour and play in their facility. While the main focus of the LaughterBoss is on the residents, a positive impact on staff, visitors and the general community has been reported. The LaughterBoss can reduce staff stress and improve morale as well as assist staff to better meet quality of life and psychosocial needs of residents. This is done through assisting communication, increased support, giving residents cognitive control, providing positive diversion and generally increasing the 'smileage' factor.

From relying on others to working alone

With the increasing presence of clowns working in healthcare, and the published research accompanying this, there has been a growing acknowledgement of the value of play and humour in healthcare. This is now finding its way into the preparatory and post-professional curricula of nurses, doctors and other allied health professionals.[33] In addition, experienced professional healthcare practitioners are now beginning to explore ways that they may integrate these clown-plays into their everyday practice. In the next section, we will start to look at basic principles that enable you to do this.

Notes

1 Much of this chapter is based on material that first appeared in Warren, B. (2010). Foolish Medicine: some connections between medieval fools and clown-doctors. *Les cahiers de l'idiotie*, Vol. 2 No. 1 pp. 145–164.
2 *Stultorum plena sunt omnia*, this maxim of Cicero can be found in Welsford, 1935, p.xi, Willeford, 1969, p.30 and Otto, 2001, whose entire book is based on this premise.
3 See Chapter 3, Clown-Play 101.
4 Worldwide, two clown-doctors do have medical degrees but they are the exception.
5 In Scotland and other parts of Europe this is yellow.
6 Hippocrates is often heralded as 'the father of modern medicine'.
7 Cotlove, 1999.
8 Billington, 1984.
9 Otto, 2001.
10 Welsford, 1935.
11 Towsen, 1976; Van Blerkom, 1995.
12 For example *The New York Times* reports Barnum and Bailey visiting children in New York hospitals in 1908.
13 Jando, 2003.
14 Killick, 2003; Meincke, 2000; Oppenheimer et al., 1997; Simonds & Warren, 2001, 2004, 2009; Spitzer, 2001, 2006; Warren, 2003, 2004, 2008a, 2008b.
15 These include Australia, Austria, Brazil, Canada, France, Germany, Israel, Italy, The Netherlands, Scotland, Switzerland, Spain and the USA.
16 'Jests' describes both physical and verbal business, and many jesters kept books, 'Jest Books', that contained all their jests. Today the word *Shtick* or *Lazzi* or *Jeu* would more usually be used to describe this. We did consider using our term 'Clown-Play' but decided to stick with the historically more appropriate term, 'Jest'.

17 Otto, 2001; Willeford, 1969.
18 Otto, 2001; Welsford, 1935.
19 Ecclesiates 1:15 in Gibbons, 1899.
20 'A frequent pastime involving jesters . . . in which one person supplied the first line and the second would complete the couplet, preferably with suitable rhymes and parallels', Otto, 2002 p.16.
21 For an example of this see Warren 2009b p.153
22 Professor David Currow has remarked, facing a life threatening illness is a time of heightened emotions and therefore there is an integral place for humour and laughter.
23 Willeford, 1969.
24 Billington, 1984; Erasmus, 1946; Otto, 2001; Towsen, 1976; Welsford, 1935; Willeford, 1969.
25 Hyde, 2000; Koller and Gryski, 2008; Meincke, 2000; Oppenheimer et al.,1997; Simonds and Warren, 2001; Spitzer, 2006, 2001; Van Blerkom, 1995; Warren, 2008, 2004, 2002.
26 Battrick, 2007.
27 Vagnoli et al., 2005; Golan et al., 2007.
28 Friedler et al., 2011.
29 Gozal et al., 2011.
30 See reference section for more extensive list of studies.
31 E.g. Killick, 2003; Spitzer, 2008; Vinit 2008; Warren, 2008b, Warren and Spitzer, 2011.
32 At this time of writing these findings are awaiting publication.
33 E.g. Peter teaches, lectures and gives one-day workshops for medical students and allied health professionals at several Australian universities as part of their curriculum.

3 Clown-Play 101[1]

Integrating clown-plays into your own practice

In this section, we will outline basic first principles for integrating play and humour into your own practice. However, we need to state what may be obvious to you that it is beyond the scope of this book for us to individualise applications of specific clown-plays to your practice.

What we provide here can be considered *risky business* as for many readers this will be stepping outside of your normal comfort zone. The rewards are worth the risk! Be patient, as most new approaches are not 100% successful the first time – 'failure is the key to success'! Taking the information provided here and adapting it to your own specific situation is in itself a creative act.

One last thing, as we are aware that physicians and many other healthcare professionals are used to working with information delivered in 'bullet point form', we have made a deliberate choice to primarily use this approach here.

Basic rules

1 Preparation and planning: 'Measure twice, cut once'

All of what follows will focus on working with patients/residents and/or clients. However, the principles, and most of the clown-plays, presented in this book can also be used in working for and with colleagues and professional staff. The activities can be used in group building and team exercises and in in-service and other training.

Preparation and planning is the key to success in any creative endeavour. Planning within your abilities and for the needs of the individuals or group with whom you work goes a long way to ensuring a successful experience for all involved. Here are some questions that should be considered in your preparation and planning before implementing clown-plays in your practice.

- Who am I and what are my strengths?
  - Whatever your strengths or interests find a way to use these:
    - If you like to tell stories or jokes with your family or you are a singer these skills can be used when implementing clown-plays
- Who am I working with?

- As we will discuss later, planning for seniors with dementia is different to working with young adults with Down's syndrome.
- Where am I working?
  - The space in which you are working affects what clown-plays you may use.
  - What is my primary job function in this context?
    - Your job description affects the way patients/clients may view you
      - You will need to consider status issues e.g. patients often perceive that there is a hierarchy between the healthcare professional (higher status) and the patient (lower status).
      - We suggest that temporarily changing status, which may be risky as it will take you out of your comfort zone, is a central principle for healthcare professionals wishing to use humour and play.
        - As an example, in the work of clown-doctors there is a constant shifting between who is 'high status' and who is 'low status' which provides opportunities to play beyond fixed roles.
- What else is happening in the 'patient' / client's life?
  - Timing is everything!
    - Choosing the right moment to introduce play is important
  - Be sensitive to the events happening so as to somehow match the clown-play to the circumstances presented
    - This is one of the principles of person-centred care.
- Being *appropriately inappropriate* –
  - While clowns throughout history have used play to question and challenge societal norms, when you implement clown-plays into your practice, you step into the world of the clown, which brings with it an element of the inappropriate.
    - Unlike the clown, you must endeavour to be *Appropriately Inappropriate*. This requires you to be aware of what is acceptable practice to the culture of your specific healthcare unit and how far you may go before crossing the line.
      - Realistically, the rules of all healthcare units are influenced by many factors, not only is this line not fixed, but it often changes 'before your very eyes'.
        - If at any point you overstep the line, never underestimate the power of apology.
  - Remember humour may be used both constructively and destructively.
    - It is important that you laugh with and not at the people with whom you are engaged.
    - Also the context in which, or the people with whom, a clown-play is employed will change how it is perceived:
      - E.g. a risqué clown-play, which an adolescent may find funny, may be seen by an older person or a person with strong religious beliefs as being inappropriate.
- Above all else, be on the look out for opportunities to instigate clown-play.

Walk before you run

- Start small
    - It is better to do 'the one thing well' than lots of plays badly.
- Choose 2–3 activities that with practice you can become comfortable with:
    - 'Repetition is the key to success'
        - Remember the play may not work as you planned first time out. Don't be disheartened. Remember the journey can be every bit as enjoyable as arriving at your destination.
    - Look for opportunities to practice
        - Practice – anywhere and everywhere e.g.:
            - At home
            - With friends
            - With co-workers
            - Waiting in line at the grocery store

2 Making appropriate choices: Questions to ask yourself

Who am I working with?

- Patients / Clients / Residents:
    - Age(s)?
        - Children
        - Adults
        - Seniors
    - Diseases Processes / Diagnoses:
        - Medical
        - Surgical
        - Life changing
        - Life threatening

Why am I choosing to use:

- A clown-play in this situation?
    - This particular clown-play?

How do I choose an appropriate clown-play?

- Context of my interactions?
    - Individual / Family– Clinical consultation – 1–4 people in the room
    - Group (Therapy) work – e.g. with 8–12 adolescents w/ eating disorders
- What types of clown play are available to me?
    - These include: Magical; Verbal; Musical; Imaginative etc.
        - For a full list see Clown-Play section (p.34)
- What are your intended outcomes?
    - These include: Building Rapport, Communication, Stress Reduction etc.
        - For a full list see Clown-Play section

When do I introduce the clown-play?

There is no single, simple or correct answer to *this* question. However factors to consider are:

- How comfortable am I with:
  - The patient and / or their family / co-workers?
  - The context I am working in?
  - The clown-play I have chosen?
- In the end while timing is everything. . . NO time is ever perfect.
  - As the great British philosopher Mary Poppins once said, ‘once begun, half done!’

How long should the clown-play last?

Knowing how to choose a play appropriate to the time available becomes easier with experience.

- We have divided clown-plays into three groups;
  - Short plays – less than five minutes;
  - Medium plays – five to ten minutes;
  - Long plays – more than ten minutes.
- The length of time available to you for each clown-play can be affected by many factors e.g.
  - The context in which you plan to implement the play;
  - The health of the patient or resident;
  - The time of day, etc.

Again simply beginning and trying things out is the simplest way to find out what works in your situation.

3 Successfully employing clown-plays in your practice

Where am I working?

There are four primary locations where you might employ clown-plays:

- Clinic / private practice
- Family home
- Residential care facility (seniors’ home / LTC / aged care / home for person with disability etc.)
- Hospital

Figure 3.1 Sad and happy

Points to consider:

- *At the bedside:* e.g. in a hospital / residential facility
    - Proximity
        - How close should I stand?
        - Asking permission may be verbal or non-verbal
            - Begins the process of engagement
- A room in a residential facility is a person's home.
    - Levels
        - Make eye contact
            - Avoid 'towering over patient'
    - Diagnosis
        - Severity of 'illness'
        - Length of stay in hospital
        - Prognosis
    - Medication
        - Will this affect communication / interactions?
    - Time of day
    - Your familiarity with 'patient'
    - What else is happening around the space
    - Age
    - Gender

- ○ Who else is in the room
  - – Familiarity one with another

- *In your consulting room*
  - Age
  - Gender
  - Reason for visit
  - Presenting symptoms
  - Familiarity one w/ another
  - Who else is in the room
  - What else is happening around the space

- *In larger rooms* (i.e. bigger than office or bedside)
  - Reason for meeting
  - Numbers in the room
    - Ages? Gender(s)?
    - Relationship to one another?
  - Set up of room
  - What else is happening around the space
  - Frequency, duration and # in sequence of meetings

- *Other spaces:*
  - It is possible to use clown-plays in almost any space e.g.:
    - Staff meeting room
    - Car parks
    - Open spaces outside

Reading the scene / the moment

- To be continually successful in employing clown-plays in your practice requires that you become a *Creative Detective.*
  - What this means is that you:
    - See yourself as an active *Change Agent*
      - Always looking for opportunities to
        - Initiate clown-play
        - Establish the value of smiles, laughter and play
          - In both word and deed
    - Are situated in the 'Here and Now'
    - See beyond 'rules and routine'
    - Are sensitive to the context in which you work
      - Perceptive to subtle changes
  - In the environment
  - In energy flow
    - Listen with *All Antennas Up*
      - I.e. use ALL your senses to gather information

    - Actively engage in each moment
      - N.B. Be open to the possibility of unexpected responses
        - This information may cause you to revise your plans and your intended outcomes

Engaging with your 'audience'

- Establish connection with patient / resident or group
  - Each time you meet, create a connection / build rapport
    - 'As if for the first time'
      - See each patient / client / resident *anew*
      - Avoid falling back on pre-set or stereotypical expectations or responses
  - Actively listen
    - Make connections between and among things in the patient / resident's life
    - Where possible integrate their story into your clown-plays especially verbal ones
- Find ways back (in) to the person
  - See them as human being in the moment i.e. do not rely on labels or diagnoses
    - Especially true when working in areas of *stroke* and *dementia*

(Playfully) reframing the interaction

- Encourage successful outcomes by being (creatively) engaged.
- Change the ways you think and see
  - The patient
  - Their family
  - The healthcare team working with them
- Motivate patient / resident to commit to and participate in treatment
  - Enhancing therapeutic:
    - Alliance – between patient and healthcare team
    - Compliance – with treatment
- Use clown-plays to reduce:
  - Stress for:
    - Patient / resident
    - Family
    - Healthcare team
  - Risk of failure
    - For patient and professional

'Failure is the key to success'

- 'Great achievements involve great risk'
  - 'It is better to beg forgiveness, than ask for permission'
- New plays often develop out of 'miscues' and 'misunderstanding the rules'
  - 'Learn the rules, so that you know how to break them properly'
- Don't compare yourself to others
  - Very little works perfectly the first time
    - 'Intuition = Innate ability + learned skills and previous experience'
      - Simply put, the more you try things out the better the experience will be, for both you and your *audience.*

4 A few more words about the power of humour in healthcare

Humour can be effectively used in a wide variety of clinical situations but it can involve risk as well as benefit. Be sensitive in selecting the content and manner of humour, as patients are often not in a place of power and may be too inhibited to express disapproval. Having empathy, respect and authenticity diminishes power imbalance and facilitates a deliberative practitioner[2]–patient relationship.

Humour in healthcare recognises that the human condition is shared by the practitioner and the patient. This kind of humour connects. It is empathetic and compassionate. It embraces rather than separates. Humour can strengthen the practitioner–patient relationship thus enhancing the effectiveness of other forms of therapy.

The use of quiet, respectful humour can give patients licence to enter personal or sensitive areas. In her palliative care work, Dean (1997) discusses the importance of humour and that it should neither be disregarded or trivialised. Humour has healing capacities even in the presence of death and dying.

In the next chapter we examine particular strategies and approaches for introducing humour and play into your practice.

Notes

1 In North America (and increasingly in the UK and Europe) an introductory course is '101'.

2 We have used the term *practitioner* to cover doctors and nurses as well as allied and other healthcare professionals.

4 Strategies and approaches

In addition to a wide range of clown-plays available to you, many of which are described later in this book, there are several different strategies and approaches that can be employed to make a room 'Sparkle and Shine'[1] or to put a smile on someone's face. What follows is a description of but a few of these.

Creating a smile-filled environment

In the early 1970s when Peter Senior, a visual artist and lecturer in Visual Arts, needed space to hang three very large murals he chose a hospital in Manchester. Hanging his murals not only brightened the mood and environment of the hospital space but it was also a major catalyst for the development of the *Manchester Hospitals Arts Project* (MHA). This simple act led to a sea change in the way that hospital environments were decorated and designed in the UK and elsewhere.[2]

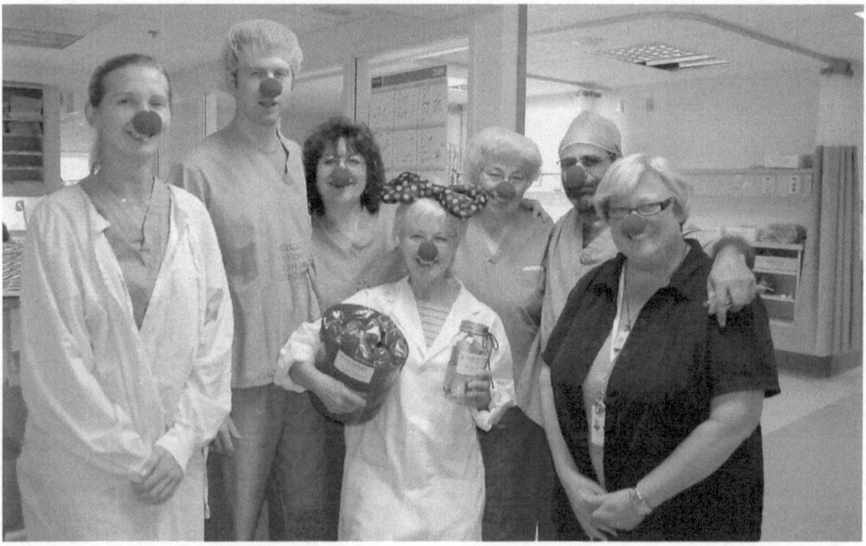

Figure 4.1 Healthcare staff noses

While some progress has been made, doctor's offices, hospitals and nursing homes are still not generally smile-inducing environments! Creating smile-filled settings starts with a conscious decision to make the room inviting and relaxing: a place in which people dealing with trauma or sickness do not have their situation compounded, by an uninviting, unfriendly and stressful space.

While much has been written on this subject and on the importance of *mood boosting decor* (there is now even a new field of study *Neuroarchitecture)* it is beyond the scope and focus of this book to dwell on this. Here we will focus on a few simple common sense, value-added elements to increase the *Smile Quotient* of the room.

Let there be light . . .

Nothing is less likely to make someone smile than a poorly lit and dark room.

- Make sure that the room is well illuminated.
- Enhance whatever natural light is available
- Limit or remove old-style fluorescents

Visual Cues

Do you know the way to . . .? Importance of signs

For some people (e.g. people who live with dementia and who wander) decor and providing good visual cues can be particularly important: For example clear signage for the following is especially important:

- Washrooms (WC / toilet / bathroom) –
    - Amusing YES! Confusing . . . NOT SO MUCH!
        - If only I had a $1 for every time I have stood bemused in front of images that give me no idea which is the men's toilet . . .!
- Entrances / exits
    - Believe it or not you can't exit through a broom closet . . . although it does amuse others!

John Zeisel suggests if you provide good visual cues – pictures and objects they're familiar with, at destinations (e.g. at the ends of hallways, such as kitchens, activity spaces) and doors that lead out into safe and inviting healing gardens – people with dementia may stop wandering and begin to walk with purpose. This will lead to less agitation and more opportunities for smiles.

On paintings and photographs: Monet a slip between cup and . . .?

Medical and professional offices are littered (this word consciously chosen!) with poor reproductions of familiar artwork and badly taken and poorly composed

Figure 4.2 Dolphin-cow

photographs. These often are humorous but not consciously so! Here are a few suggestions:

- Hang good quality paintings or pictures. Try to make these the best you can afford.
  - We suggest conventional or representational pieces that do not leave the viewer scratching their head or disturbed! I.e. tranquil, pastoral or colour-filled
    - However it is probably better to hang aunt Mildred's one of a kind watercolour of your local pond than a poorly reproduced copy of Monet's Garden
- You could also hang a single conversation *piece*
  - A picture that makes the viewer do a double take e.g.

Humour Noticeboard

This is a passive installation suitable in most healthcare practices and that invites humour.

- A Humour Board should be strategically placed.
  - One person is needed to maintain and supervise this space

Figure 4.3 Humour Notice Board

- ◦ However, anyone (colleagues, patients, residents, families and staff) can be encouraged to bring jokes / humour articles/photos etc.

Objets d'art

Strategically placing clown dolls, soft toys, sculptures and other items can create both conversation and opportunities for play.

Humour Carts and Baskets

Here are a few simple ways to lighten up an environment to increase the Smile Quotient of a room.

- *Humour Cart / Basket* is, like a Humour Board, another opportunity of introducing play and creating smiles. It is in itself a play resource.
  - ◦ A basket, strategically placed, can have a variety of colourful props such as scarves, wigs, hats, lightweight balls, Polaroid camera / pictures, puppets, magic, balloons etc., ready to be used at a moment's notice.
    - – A cart should be on wheels. Just like a medication trolley that dispenses medicine, a humour trolley brings smiles.
    - – Local businesses and community groups can be approached to donate equipment for the cart/basket.

Using clothing and costumes to brighten up lives and put smiles on faces

One simple technique to create smiles is to wear an eye-catching or unexpected piece of clothing, a costume or a clothing accessory. Here are a few examples of how to make simple changes to the way you look to create smiles and change your environment.

Wearing a hat or headpiece[3]

This is a strategy that both men and women can use. A hat can completely change the shape of your face. Hats can be simple or flamboyant. They can suggest people (e.g. Sherlock Holmes' deerstalker[4]) or places (a beret – France). There are so many different hats to choose from that it is possible to have several different hats each chosen for different occasions or intended outcomes.

Here is a sample of the many hats and headpieces to choose from:

- Tiara / crown;
- Pirate hat;
- Bandana / brightly coloured head scarf;
- Deerstalker / Panama / Pork Pie hats;
- Safari / Tilley hat;

Figure 4.4 Hats

- French beret;
- Large brimmed Ascot style hat;
- Hats with feathers;
- Fool's hat – cap with bells / pointed dunce cap etc.

***Wearing a necktie*[5]**

As a general rule, men more usually wear ties. This means that when women do wear them, they can create smiles and/or raise eyebrows. Ties can be strategically chosen to raise a smile or change the mood of an interaction. Both of us have several different colourful and eye-catching ties which we use either to brighten up what we are wearing and/or the faces of people looking at us. Bernie's favourite tie is reversible with multi-coloured paw prints on one side and multi-coloured cats on the other, while Peter has a smiling clown adorning a multi-coloured silk tie.

Wearing brightly coloured 'everyday' clothes

By-and-large, women have so many more choices when it comes to clothing. However, in professional environments, with the possible exception of *Dress Down Fridays,* the range and colour palette of clothes chosen is very limited. Wearing a brightly coloured large patterned shirt or blouse changes the way you are looked at. Deliberately mixing and matching opposing colours (e.g. bright greens with lurid purples) or patterns (e.g. polka dots with checks) can create amused responses.

Adding a clothing accessory to your regular wardrobe

This is another simple technique that can change how people interact with you. Wearing Wonder Woman bracelets (which from time to time you strike together to make yourself invisible (see *Stupid Magic* (p.81)) or a feather boa are possible additions. Simpler still are eye-catching broaches, necklaces or other jewellery pieces. Finally, do not forget the smallest mask, and a clown's *secret weapon* – the red nose. Wearing this simple adornment, while merely standing still doing nothing, almost always creates instant merriment and smiles!

Wearing a costume piece or 'costume'

A single costume piece like a decorated pirate's eye patch or a Harry Potter style *invisibility cloak* can often bring a smile, especially if once again you use *Stupid Magic* (p.81) to make yourself 'invisible'. Dressing up in full costume (e.g. as Wonder Woman, Batman or a medieval fool) is always an option, BUT timing and context have to be carefully thought through.[6] However, used sparingly either of these simple strategies can be employed as a positive way of creating inquiring looks and smiling faces.

Wearing a clown nose

A clown nose changes the shape and look of your face. While many people may think that clown noses come in one style, a round red nose, they are available in many different shapes, colours and sizes.[7] You do not have to do anything, simply put the nose on and smile!

Putting on a clown nose, what Jacques Le Coq called the smallest mask in the world, almost always puts a smile on the face of the people looking at you.[8] Now, even when doing the most mundane or difficult tasks, simply by wearing your clown nose you will change others' perceptions of these and of you.

A word of caution: when wearing your nose you must be careful not to get lost in its seductiveness. For like all masks, wearing a nose can occasionally take on a life of its own sometimes creating a new persona for you without you realising it. Only wear your nose for short periods at a time. If you feel yourself getting lost in the 'mask', take your nose off and say out loud significant information about yourself e.g. your name, age, where you live, names of your cat, dog, spouse etc.

Working with a prop

Simple options include a 'magic' wand, a squeaker or a mouth whistle (such as can be removed from squeaky pet toys) and puppets (see *Finger Puppets* p.99). Props, once animated, often have a life of their own but do not forget their value as a communication tool to engage with patients, residents and others.

Working with squeakers

Squeakers are essential equipment for clowns. They come in many different shapes and sizes. Most are small enough to hide in your hand, a pocket or other areas of clothing. Clowns carry them in the waistband of their trousers or underpants and female clowns often secrete them inside their bra. Playing with a squeaker does take a little practice but can have a magical quality (See *Squeaky Magic* p.82)

Working with 'found' objects

Imagination is key to transforming any object from its *functional* to its *fantastical* uses. Konstantin Stanislavski (the great theatre director and actor trainer) had an exercise where he asked his students to find different uses for a shoe (often referred to as *1001 things to do with a shoe*).[9]

Possibilities for objects that can be used and transformed abound in any room. These can range from dishtowels or pieces of paper to more elaborate things e.g. a toilet plunger, a walking stick, a turkey baster or a Fool's carved bauble. The only limits to the possible uses of each object are your own imagination.

Using song and music to change mood and engage communication

Our lives are enmeshed in story, and song has been one of the primary vehicles by which human beings have told their tales and passed on their history and wisdom to others. Even today throughout our lives, music and song surround us. These songs and melodies are the backdrop against which we live our lives. There are the melodies that are sung to us as young children that were the cornerstones and signposts to our transformations into adulthood and those that we hum and sing along to as we age. They are not only the cultural wallpaper against which we carry out our day to day transactions, but also this music acts as markers for significant events that make up the life story for each of us individually. These words and tunes accompany and anchor important events in our lives and often trigger memories when these same pieces of music are re-encountered.

For centuries, music has been an essential element of human communities for communicating history and helping to pass the time. In the past, people at work, from sailors to members of chain gangs, have sung songs and hummed melodies, to help reduce the monotony of their job and/or as the rhythmic reinforcement of the actions needed to complete the task at hand.

In modern times, musicians and music therapists have used music to help change individuals' moods and to help them relax. While aptitude and skill are most certainly important if you wish to be a professional musician or music therapist, however, you do not have to be a musician or a singer to integrate music and song into your work place, especially if your goal is to have fun and help people to smile.[10]

There are so many ways that music and song, both live and *canned*,[11] can be used to help create smiles. Here are a few ideas for ways that music can be used:

- *Music as a catalyst for activity*: Songs can be employed as stimulus for, or as an accompaniment to, any interaction or task
  - E.g. Singing well-known songs *a cappella* or using an iPhone / Mp3 / CD player during rehabilitation therapy
- *Music to change the mood*
  - E.g. using soothing music while conducting an invasive procedure
- *Music as Communitas* e.g.
  - Singing together – simple songs like 'You are my Sunshine' or 'When you're Smiling', almost never fail to bring a smile
  - Using the clown-play *Song Circle* (p.71) or *Juggling Tunes* (p.72) for group building
  - Singing familiar songs to change a mood, to help relax or to amuse.
  - Using the clown-play *Stump the Chump* (p.74) where you, or a patient/ client, offer a word or phrase and sing a song that either begins with it or contains it.
- *Music purely for laughter*
  - Coaxing music out of everyday objects:

  - A kazoo or comb and paper are the obvious examples but there are other possibilities e.g. using a large bore surgical syringe as a 'Swanee whistle'
- Nonsense songs:
  - Made up songs using animal sounds
  - Gibberish or nonsensical words and phrases sung to the tunes of well-known songs (*see Cats and Dogs*, p.75)
- Situational songs:
  - Use of snippets, phrases and words of a song as a filler, mood changer or response e.g. sing a couple of lines from a song that includes a phrase or comment spoken by a patient or healthcare worker.

In the next sections of the book, we present a selection of clown-plays described in detail and also an at-a-glance grid which easily allows you to choose a clown-play for a particular situation.

Notes

1 A term attributed to Michael Christensen.
2 Peter Senior and his work with MHA was major influence on the later development of the *Arts In Hospitals* and *Arts for Health* movement worldwide.
3 Novelty hats are available from many sites e.g.:
http://www.alibaba.com/showroom/novelty-hats.html
http://donshobbyshop.ca/index.php?page=categories/index.php&catid=1350
4 Although I believe, Conan Doyle never referred to Holmes wearing a deerstalker; this was an addition made by Basil Rathbone.
5 Novelty neckties are available from many sites e.g.:
http://stores.ebay.com.au/PMC-PARTY-SUPPLIES/NOVELTY-NECKTIES-/_i.html?_fsub=4849856015
http://www.zazzle.com.au/novelty+ties
6 There are obviously certain days of the year where this is more acceptable than others (e.g. Halloween in North America). If you work in a setting where people are 'at risk' or frail it may be best, at the very least, to discuss this idea with a co-worker or supervisor before 'jumping in and filling both wellies'.
7 There are several places from which you can order both foam and professional clown noses e.g. http://www.justclownnoses.com/; or
http://www.juggleart.com/catalog/index.php?cPath=158_102; http://www.firetoys.co.uk/juggling/circus/clown-noses.html and for foam noses only: http://www.graftobian.com/commerce/catalog.jsp?catId=2109 or
8 The only caveat would be not to wear a clown nose around people who suffer from *coulrophobia*, morbid fear of clowns.
9 See *Magic Newspaper* (p.83), which is a variation on this and a very good starting point for thinking beyond the functional uses of 'found' objects.
10 A 'fact' that more and more reality singing competitions bear out!
11 Canned music refers to any recorded music.

5 Key to clown-plays

Introduction

In this section, we present more than 50 clown-plays for use in your practice. The activities are divided into seven sections:

- Name
- Verbal
- Physical
- Musical
- Imaginative
- Magical
- Miscellaneous

All of the plays are described in detail. We have also identified elements related to successfully implementing each of them and the potential benefits that may accrue from playing them.

In presenting these plays we have provided a Key: this is used as a shorthand throughout the description of the games and the At-a-Glance Grid, which serves as a quick index.

WHO

- *Anyone / Any Group*:
    - Many plays can be used with almost any one. However the focus will be different for the following:
- *Patients / Clients / Residents:*
    - When working with these individuals the plays are usually value added to an already determined goal or treatment path.
        - Obviously working with seniors with dementia is different to working with adolescents.
- *Professionals / Staff*:
    - When working with professional colleagues the plays are usually presented in a workshop setting or may be introduced on the fly, or as an *Ambush of the Intellect*.

DURATION

- Short (under 5mins)
- Medium (5–10mins)
- Long (10+)

AGE

- Children
    - Many of the plays presented here are one-on-one in the consulting room or at the bedside
- Adolescents (13–17)
- Adults
- Seniors (65+)
- All Ages

INTERACTION

- Individual / Family
    - 1–4 people in the room
- Group work
    - 5+ people

LOCATION

- Bedside
- Consulting room
- Activity room[1]
- Outside
- Anywhere

BENEFITS

All plays are intended to induce smiles / laughter and / or playfulness.

Any play may provide you with new information that can inform person-centred care and future goal and/or treatment plans.

In addition the following benefits are also possible:

- **Ice Breaker –** Great way to start the session and help make connections
- **Imagination** – Opportunity to exercise creativity and/or spontaneity and /or imagination
- **Rapport Builder** – Strengthens relationship(s) between practitioner and patient(s) / resident(s) / client(s)
- **Communication** – Enhances inter-personal communication
- **Stress Reduction –** Helps reduce stress, often through release of anger, frustration, anxiety etc.
- **Diversionary** – Distraction from problem / procedure / situation
- **Group Building –** Strengthens relationships amongst participants

- **Sensitivity** – To others and / or surroundings
- **Physical** – Enhances breathing / vocalisation and / or physical control and / or increases body awareness
- **Memory** – May help recall of past experiences and emotions

One other note: there is always room for *Spontaneous Play*: an on the spur of the moment opportunity, not connected to any predetermined goal(s) or treatment plan, to inject play and laughter into a situation just because it is fun. Observations and experiences gained from this *Spontaneous Play* may inform your future interactions with your patients, clients and even your colleagues.

Notes

1 Activity Room may describe any large open meeting space suitable for group activities e.g. residents' lounge, a chapel, gym, workshop space, common room etc. Be advised that clown-plays are likely to be noisy.

6 Clown-plays

1 This Is My Name & How I Feel About It

Who:	Anyone / Any Group
Number of players:	5+
Ages:	Any Age
Equipment:	Chairs are useful but not essential
Duration:	Short to Medium Play
Where:	Activity / Common Room
When:	At the very beginning of a group

How:	• Participants stand in a circle facing each other
	• Each person introduces themself by saying their first name and sharing some information about it e.g.
	  ○ The meaning of the name e.g. Bernard – means Heart of the Bear
	  ○ Who they were named after/for
	  ○ Why that name was chosen
	  ○ How they feel about their name
	• Each person finishes by saying: 'My name is. . .'
	Length of time will be related to number of people in the group.

Benefits:	Ice Breaker, Group Building, Rapport, Sensitivity, Memory
Safety, Risks or Difficulties:	Difficulty – some people feel awkward about speaking in public May lead to discussions about: Family history and dynamics Heritage and ethnicity and Religious beliefs

Limits:	
Adaptations:	Can be adapted for use with individual Patient / Resident at the Bedside or in the Consulting room.
Other considerations:	Encourages active listening
Variations:	• Participants can talk about their FULL name. • Ask each person to tell a story about themself that involves the use of their name. *ECHO* : • When everyone has finished speaking have each person say their name out loud followed by everyone else in the group repeating it.

2 Where I Played as a Child

Who:	Anyone / Any Group
Number of players:	10+
Ages:	Adolescents, Adults, Seniors
Equipment:	Chairs are useful but not essential
Duration:	Short to Medium Play
Where:	Activity / Common Room
When:	Consider this early to middle of group activity.
How:	• This activity is done in a group. • Each person speaks for 2-3 minutes about where, when and with whom they played as a child. After everyone has spoken the leader may decide to have a group discussion.
Benefits:	Memory, Sensitivity, Rapport, Communication
Safety, Risks or Difficulties:	
Limits:	
Adaptations:	
Other considerations:	• This exercise recalls play, memory and positive experiences. • Bringing past memories to the present. • This is also about sharing an experience without judgment. • Everyone experiences telling a story and being a listener/observer. Works well after *Remembering Childhood Play*
Variations:	

3 Meetings & Greetings

Who:	Any Group
Number of players:	6+
Ages:	Adolescents, Adults, Seniors
Equipment:	
Duration:	Short to Medium Play
Where:	Activity / Common Room
	Can be played outdoors
When:	Early in group activity.

How:	• Participants spread out around the room.
	• Leader asks group to explore several different ways to meet others in the group, One variant at a time
	• Examples of greeting include:
	  ○ Hand shake while saying 'Hello I'm (name). . .'
	  ○ Hug
	  ○ Kiss(es) on the cheek(s)
	  ○ Rubbing noses
	  ○ Bow / curtsy
	  ○ Hi five
	Leader can then ask group for other suggestions

Benefits:	Ice Breaker, Imagination, Group Building, Communication, Rapport Builder
Safety, Risks or Difficulties:	Some people may feel uncomfortable with some of the greetings
Limits:	May be problematic for people who are 'touch phobic' or from ethnic groups with prohibitions on physical touching between sexes
Adaptations:	Can be followed by a discussion about cultural norms
Other considerations:	
Variations:	*HELLO / GOOD BYE* Working in pairs, participants are asked to walk towards and away from each other finding as many different ways of saying hello and good bye as they can *EXITS / ENTRANCES* Working in pairs, participants are asked to finding as many different ways of entering and exiting a room as they can

4 Remembering Childhood Play

Who:	Any Group
Number of players:	2+
Ages:	Adolescents, Adults, Seniors
Equipment:	Chairs an asset but not essential
Duration:	Medium Play
Where:	Anywhere (Can be played outside)
When:	Consider this early to middle of group activity.
How:	• This activity is done in pairs. • Participants face each other. • One person tells a story of a pleasant childhood memory play. This can be real or imagined. • The partner watches facial expressions but does not talk. After a couple of minutes the role is reversed for another couple of minutes.
Benefits:	Communication, Sensitivity, Rapport, Memory
Safety, Risks or Difficulties:	Only positive and pleasant memories to be expressed.
Limits:	
Adaptations:	
Other considerations:	• This exercise recalls play, memory and positive experiences. • Bringing past memories to the present. • Everyone experiences telling a story and being a listener / observer. • This is also about sharing an experience without judgment. • Good photo opportunity
Variations:	Can be followed by: *Where I Played as a Child* (p.36)

5 It Makes Me Happy When. . .

Who:	Anyone / Any Group
Number of players:	2+
Ages:	Adolescents, Adults, Seniors
Equipment:	Chairs are useful but not essential
Duration:	Short to Medium Play
Where:	Anywhere
When:	Consider this early to middle of group activity.
How:	• This activity is done in pairs.
	• Participants sit facing each other.
	• Each person is given 1–2 minutes to talk about anything (events, TV shows, puppies / kittens at play) that makes them smile or laugh.
	• Their partner watches and actively listens, but does not talk.
	• After a couple of minutes the role is reversed for another couple of minutes.
	The pair is allowed 5+ minutes to discuss each other's comments.
Benefits:	Imagination, Communication, Sensitivity, Rapport Builder
Safety, Risks or Difficulties:	N/A. Only positive and pleasant memories to be expressed.
Limits:	Can be adapted for older children (8+)
Adaptations:	
Other considerations:	This exercise provides participants the opportunity to exercise 'active listening' and empathy.

Variations:	• Pairs can we asked to rejoin the circle to share their partner's stories with the group
	• Pairs can be asked to talk about what makes them sad / cry / angry
	• Task can be simplified, pairs can be asked to talk about your favourite:
	  ◦ Comedian
	  ◦ TV show
	  ◦ Romantic comedy / comic film

6 If You Could Have Dinner with Anyone . . .

Who:	Any Group
Number of players:	6+
Ages:	Adolescents, Adults, Seniors
Equipment:	Chairs are useful but not essential
Duration:	Short to Medium Play
Where:	Any space that will accommodate pairs. Can be indoors / outdoors
When:	Consider this early to middle of group activity.
How:	• This activity is done in pairs. • Participants sit facing each other. • Each person is asked to tell their partner, ◦ 'If you could have dinner with anyone who would it be, where would you go and why?' • Their partner watches and actively listens, but does not talk. After a couple of minutes the role is reversed for another couple of minutes.
Benefits:	Communication, Sensitivity, Rapport Builder, Imagination
Safety, Risks or Difficulties:	N/A. Fantasy stories can become 'risqué' especially with adolescents
Limits:	May be inappropriate for persons with difficulties dealing with reality
Adaptations:	
Other considerations:	This exercise provides participants the opportunity to exercise 'active listening' and thinking creatively 'in the moment'
Variations:	Pairs can we asked to rejoin the circle to share their partner's stories with the group

	• Empty Chair:
	   ◦ Ask for a volunteer
	   ◦ Ask them to imagine their dinner guest is sitting in an empty chair
	   ◦ Tell them to ask their most important question to their guest
	   ◦ Now ask them to sit in the chair and reply AS their guest

7 If I Could Be Anywhere in the World

Who:	Any Group
Number of players:	10+
Ages:	Adolescents, Adults, Seniors
Equipment:	Chairs are useful but not essential
Duration:	Short to Medium Play (depending on size of the group)
Where:	Any space that will accommodate pairs. Can be indoors / outdoors
When:	Consider this early to middle of group activity.
How:	• This activity is done in pairs. • Participants sit facing each other. • Each person is asked to tell their partner, ◦ 'If you could be anywhere in the world right now, where would you be and why?' • Their partner watches and actively listens, but does not talk. • After a couple of minutes the role is reversed for another couple of minutes.
Benefits:	Communication, Rapport, Imagination, Sensitivity
Safety, Risks or Difficulties: Limits:	Fantasy stories can become 'risqué', especially with adolescents. May be inappropriate for persons with difficulties dealing with reality.
Adaptations:	
Other considerations:	This exercise provides participants the opportunity to exercise 'active listening' and thinking creatively 'in the moment'.
Variations:	Pairs can we asked to rejoin the circle to share their partner's stories with the group.

8 You'll Never Believe this But. . .

Who:	Anyone / Any Group
Number of players:	2+
Ages:	Adolescents, Adults and Seniors
Equipment:	Chairs are useful but not essential
Duration:	Medium Play
Where:	Any space that will accommodate pairs. Can be indoors / outdoors.
When:	Consider this early to middle of group activity.
How:	• This activity is done in pairs. • Participants sit facing each other. • Each person is given 2+ minutes to tell a personal story that begins 'You'll never believe this but. . .' ◦ The one rule is NONE of the story they tell is true! It is a complete fabrication made up as they speak. • Their partner watches and actively listens, but does not talk. • After a couple of minutes the role is reversed for another couple of minutes. • The pair is allowed 5+ minutes to discuss each other's comments.
Benefits:	Communication, Imagination, Rapport Building, Sensitivity
Safety, Risks or Difficulties:	N/A. Fantasy stories can become 'risqué'
Limits:	May be inappropriate for persons with difficulties dealing with reality
Adaptations:	Pairs can we asked to rejoin the circle to share their partner's stories with the group
Other considerations:	This exercise provides participants the opportunity to exercise 'active listening' and thinking creatively 'in the moment'
Variations:	

9 What Am I Holding?

Who:	This exercise is suitable for both clients and professionals.
Number of players:	2+
Ages:	Any Age
Equipment:	Assortment of everyday objects (cups, dishes, brush, etc.)
Duration:	Medium Play
Where:	Anywhere
When:	After *What Am I Building?* (p.44)
How:	• A and B sit back to back, in front of A is an everyday object e.g. A cup or a knife • A has to describe the object to B without telling him its name
Benefits:	Communication, Sensitivity, Physical
Safety, Risks or Difficulties:	
Limits:	
Adaptations:	Can be played seated
Other considerations:	

Variations:	• Architect and builder communicate in different languages e.g.:
	  ○ A speaks only in Spanish
	  ○ B only speaks in Hindi

10 Architect & Builder: What Am I Building?

Who:	Any Group
Number of players:	2+
Ages:	Any Ages
Equipment:	Variety of blocks of different shapes and colours.
Duration:	Medium Play
Where:	Anywhere.
When:	This activity should follow introductory and warm up activities.
How:	• 2 people sit back to back • In front of them each is an identical set of differently coloured shapes e.g. Blue triangles, red squares etc. • A has to make a shape with the blocks • As A makes the shape he tells B • B tries to copy A At the end A and B compare shapes
Benefits:	Communication, Sensitivity, Physical
Safety, Risks or Difficulties:	
Limits: **Adaptations:**	Can be played seated to accommodate people who use wheelchairs. All blocks are placed on a small table in front of the 'architect' and the 'builder'
Other considerations:	Audience often laughs loudly!

Variations:	• Architect and builder communicate in different languages e.g.:
	  ◦ Architect speaks only French
	  ◦ Builder only speaks German

11 Yes / No Story

Who:	Anyone / Any Group
Number of players:	2+
Ages:	Adolescents, Adults, Seniors
Equipment:	Chairs are useful but not essential
Duration:	Short to Medium Play
Where:	Anywhere
When:	Consider this early to middle of group activity.
How:	• This activity is done in pairs. • Participants stand or sit facing each other. • One person starts to tell their partner a made up story one line at a time • At the end of each line the storyteller looks at their partner for confirmation ◦ If partner says 'yes' then storyteller continues ◦ If they say 'NO' the storyteller has to change the line • Example: ◦ *Storyteller*: 'Once upon a time there was a blue goldfish'; ◦ *Listener*: 'NO'; ◦ *S*: ' . . . a green goldfish?; ◦ *L*: 'No'; ◦ *S*: a pink rabbit; ◦ *L*: 'YES' . . . ◦ *S*: ' A pink rabbit who had the most beautiful diamond tiara'; ◦ *L*: 'YES' After a couple of minutes the storyteller's role is reversed for another couple of minutes.
Benefits:	Imagination, Rapport Building, Communication, Sensitivity
Safety, Risks or Difficulties:	N/A. Fantasy stories can become 'risqué' especially with adolescents
Limits:	May be inappropriate for persons with difficulties dealing with reality
Adaptations:	

Other considerations:	This exercise provides participants the opportunity to exercise 'active listening' and thinking creatively 'in the moment'
Variations:	Partners can walk around the room side-by-side telling their stories.

12 Chair Warm Up

Who:	Any Group
Number of players:	2+
Ages:	Any Age
Equipment:	Chairs
Duration:	Short to Medium Play
Where:	In a large open space that will accommodate both the participants and the chairs
When:	At the beginning of a session
How:	• Everyone sits in a circle facing inwards • Play a selection of music with a melodic beat • Allow participants to dance to it, anything at all as long as they stay connected to their chair
Benefits:	Physical, Stress Reduction, Group Building
Safety, Risks or Difficulties:	Participants need to take precautions while using the chairs, and not use them inappropriately in a way that could hurt themselves or someone else. May be a few problems for people who have had a stroke.
Limits:	
Adaptations:	
Other considerations:	
Variations:	*Follow My Dance*[1] • Each participant takes it in turns to briefly lead the group – all other participants copy their movements

13 Counting Fingers

Who:	Any Group
Number of players:	Groups of 3
Ages:	10+
Equipment:	
Duration:	Short Play
Where:	Any space that accommodates the circle.
When:	Can work well at any point in group activity.
How:	• 3 Participants stand in a circle facing each other • Forming a single closed fist they move the arm up and down in unison counting out aloud . . .1, 2, 3. On the 4th (and downward) move, each person exposes any of 1 to 5 digits. ○ Together the numbers need to add up to 11. • When this happens the group, being so successful, lets out yelps of delight.
Benefits:	Ice Breaker, Rapport Builder, Communication, Group Building, Stress Reduction
Safety, Risks or Difficulties:	Difficulty – working together non-verbally
Limits:	
Adaptations:	Can be adapted for wheelchairs or seated groups with appropriate angling of chairs Limit each group to 3 people. If there are more than 3 then they become observers. This will still be fun.
Other considerations:	Can get noisy. Watch for smiles and facial expression changes.

Figure 6.1 Counting Fingers

Variations:	Once 11 is reached, Instruct groups to use both hands.
	• Now any number of digits from 1 to 10 can be exposed.
	  ◦ The aim is for the group to reach 21.
	    – Again yelps of delight are in order.

14 Dancing Fingers

Who:	Any Group
Number of players:	Any number – in pairs
Ages:	Adolescents and Adults
Equipment:	
Duration:	Short Play
Where:	Anywhere
When:	At any time.
How:	• Pair stands facing each other. Both extend their right arm forward so that your fingers are just touching your partner's. This gives the right separation. • Lower your extended arm to the side and stand relaxed. • Now both partners close their eyes. • Now slowly make a pointing gesture and begin to extend the same arm. • Slowly move the arm. The aim is to continue until the fingertips make a connection, which is then held. Without looking and without talking, the fingertips move to make a drawing in the air. One person can lead and the other follows. The lead can change.
Benefits:	Physical, Rapport Builder, Communication, Sensitivity
Safety, Risks or Difficulties:	If the play is prolonged, some people may have difficulty keeping their arm extended.
Limits:	Not suitable for people who use wheelchairs or who have significant physical restrictions
Adaptations:	May be adapted for seniors and others by using chairs.
Other considerations:	Good non-verbal link and play at beginning of workshops. Best in experiential workshop setting. Onlookers also benefit.
Variations:	• Can be done in sitting position • Music can be added.

15 Mirror Face

Who:	Any Group
Number of players:	2+, working in pairs
Ages:	Any Age
Equipment:	
Duration:	Short Play
Where:	Anywhere
When:	Anytime
How:	• Participants stand facing one another. • Partner A makes a face, e.g. a happy face. Partner B copies this facial expression as best they can. • Then Partner B makes a different face e.g. an angry face. Partner A tries to copy this new facial expression. This continues for a few turns with each taking the lead.
Benefits:	Ice Breaker, Sensitivity, Communication, Stress Reduction
Safety, Risks or Difficulties:	
Limits:	Ability to follow instructions.
Adaptations:	

Figure 6.2 Mirror Face

Other considerations:	Enhances non-verbal communication through facial expressions. Can be used as a 'memory jog' at next consult: e.g. 'do you remember the last face we made? Can you show it to me ?'
Variations:	

16 Change Three Things

Who:	Any Group
Number of players:	2+, working in pairs
Ages:	Any Age
Equipment:	
Duration:	Short Play
Where:	Any space that accommodates the circle.
When:	Anytime
How:	• Stand facing your partner. Observe each other. • Turn to face away from one another. • Partner A changes 3 things. Then A tells B to turn round to face each other. • Partner B tries to identify the 3 changes. • Now it's Partner B's turn to make changes.
Benefits:	Communication, Sensitivity, Rapport Building
Safety, Risks or Difficulties:	
Limits:	Ability to see.
Adaptations:	Can be adapted for wheelchairs or seated groups
Other considerations:	Enhances observational skills
Variations:	

17 Boat Race

Who:	Any Group
Number of players:	4+
Ages:	Adolescents and Adults
Equipment:	
Duration:	Short Play
Where:	Any open space with a carpeted or clean floor
When:	Any time
How:	• Split into two (or more) groups of equal size • In your group everyone has to mime rowing in sync with each other • The winner is the 1st boat to go 30 seconds rowing while not breaking synchronicity or moving forwards. • If any person gets out of sync the boat has to start over again
Benefits:	Group Building, Physical, Stress Reduction
Safety, Risks or Difficulties:	People must be comfortable being touched May be problematic for people who are 'touch phobic' or from ethnic groups with prohibitions on physical touching between sexes
Limits:	Not suitable for people who use wheelchairs or who have significant physical restrictions
Adaptations:	May be adapted for seniors and others by using chairs.
Other considerations:	
Variations:	• The boats move, by participants shuffling / sliding on their bottoms in unison, towards a pre-determined finish line. • The first boat there is the winner • NB this is VERY strenuous!

18 Walk Across the Room

Who:	Any Group
Number of players:	6+
Ages:	Any Age
Equipment:	
Duration:	Short to Medium Play
Where:	Activity / Common Room
When:	Anytime
How:	• All line up against one wall • Guess how many steps it will take to reach the other side • Walk across the space counting your steps • 'Were you right?', have another try
Benefits:	Physical, Group Building, Communication
Safety, Risks or Difficulties:	No more than 3 people moving at once Make sure no obstacles are in the way ESPECIALLY if people are moving backwards or with their eyes closed.
Limits:	Not suitable for people who use wheelchairs or who have severe problems with balance.
Adaptations:	Can be adapted to include people who use wheelchairs. • Now the questions is how many revolutions rather than steps
Other considerations:	

Variations:	• Move as if using a walking frame or sticks.
	• Fix eyes on a single point on opposite wall. Go to it using different movements
	  ○ Direct – Shortest direct path but can be high, low, slow, or fast
	  ○ Zig zag – Indirect route
	  ○ Backwards
	  ○ Eyes closed

19 Break My Balance

Who:	Any Group
Number of players:	2+
Ages:	Adolescents and Adults
Equipment:	
Duration:	Short Play
Where:	Any open space that fits the group size.
When:	Probably works best early in a session after group has met a couple of times but not as the first activity of the day.

How:	• Work in pairs
	• Stand facing one another
	    ○ Each with their feet together
	    ○ About arm's length away from each other
	    ○ Extend your arms out straight until your palms are level with your partner's
	• Keeping connected to your partner try to move them off balance by:
	    ○ Pushing (gently)
	    ○ Feinting
	Until one partner is knocked off balance

Benefits:	Physical, Communication, Sensitivity
Safety, Risks or Difficulties:	It is important to lay down safety rules about the degree of physical contact
Limits:	Not suitable for people who use wheelchairs or who have significant physical restrictions
Adaptations:	Can be used with older children (8yrs +) However safety rules must be strongly stressed and repeated
Other considerations:	Partners should be paired up with someone approximately of equal size.
Variations:	

20 Are You There Moriarty?

Who:	Any Group
Number of players:	2+
Ages:	Adolescents and Adults
Equipment:	2 Balloons and 2 Blindfolds
Duration:	Short Play
Where:	Activity / Common Room
When:	Probably works best early in a session after group has met a couple of times but not as the first activity of the day.

How:	• Work in pairs
	• Partners stand facing each other an arm's length
	    ◦ In their right hand they hold a balloon
	    ◦ They hold each other's left hand as if to shake it
	        – Partner A asks ' Are you there Moriarty?'
	        – Partner B replies 'I am Here'
	    ◦ Partner A then tries to strike partner B with their balloon
	        – The process is reversed with Partner B now asking ' Are you . . .'
	The game continues until one partner has scored 3 'hits'

Benefits:	Physical, Communication, Sensitivity
Safety, Risks or Difficulties:	It is important to lay down safety rules about the degree of physical contact allowed
Limits:	Not suitable for people who have significant physical restrictions or who have blood clotting disorders
Adaptations:	Can be adapted for people who use wheelchairs Can be used with older children (8yrs +) However safety rules must be strongly stressed and repeated
Other considerations:	Partners should be paired up with someone approximately of equal size. Can get VERY physical

Variations:	• A blindfold may be used
	• Instead of standing, partners:
	    ◦ lie face down with their eyes closed
	    ◦ sit on chairs

21 Dancing Cheek to Cheek

Who:	Any Group
Number of players:	2+
Ages:	Adolescents and Adults
Equipment:	
Duration:	Short Play
Where:	Anywhere
When:	Any time Works well after *Chair Warm Up* (p.47) or *Hand Dance* (p.59)
How:	• Working in pairs ∘ Play a variety of music with a good melodic beat (Pop, Celtic or Dance) – Making a mix with a variety of music works well • Partners dance – cheek to cheek ∘ i.e. connected by their buttocks! Pairs create their own dances to the music
Benefits:	Physical, Stress Reduction, Communication
Safety, Risks or Difficulties:	May be problematic for people who are 'touch phobic' or from ethnic groups with prohibitions on physical touching between sexes
Limits:	Not suitable for people who use wheelchairs or who have significant physical restrictions
Adaptations:	CONTACT DANCE is adaptable for people who use a wheelchair
Other considerations:	
Variations:	• *GROUP BOTTOM DANCE;* Dance with Anyone in the group ∘ *CONTACT DANCE* – Pairs move to music while connecting using other body parts e.g.: – shoulder to shoulder – head to head – forearm to forearm

22 Mirror Work

Who:	Anyone / Any Group
Number of players:	2+
Ages:	Any Age
Equipment:	
Duration:	Short to Medium Play
Where:	Anywhere
When:	Makes for a good warm up exercise or can be used at any time.
How:	• Played in pairs • Partners face one another approximately a hand-shake distance apart • Partner A is the 'Mirror', Partner B stands in front of the Mirror • Each partner raises both hands to chest height and so that their palms lightly touch their partner's ◦ Partner B tries to mirror A's movements • Partners take turns leading, following • Start with simple tasks e.g. brushing teeth, combing hair, shaving • Move on to more complex operations e.g. getting dressed, baking bread, etc.
Benefits:	Physical, Coordination, Communication
Safety, Risks or Difficulties:	Be sure to clear area of any tripping hazard when people have their eyes closed!
Limits:	
Adaptations:	
Other considerations:	Enhances non-verbal communication

Variations:	*HAND DANCE*
	• Partners' palms lightly touch
	• Leader plays easy to follow rhythmic music
	• Pairs move hands to the music
	  ◦ Repeat but with eyes closed
	• Advanced
	  ◦ Pairs keep their eyes closed
	  ◦ Eyes still closed they move together through the space

23 Getting the Clap – Standing Ovation

Who:	Any Group
Number of players:	10 to 30
Ages:	Adult
Equipment:	
Duration:	Short Play
Where:	Anywhere
When:	At any time
How:	• This exercise is built into and explained during the 'housekeeping' announcement at the very beginning of a workshop. • Here is the background explanation: As healthcare professionals, we are very good at giving. This activity is about receiving. • Everyone during the workshop does this activity once. • Here is the announcement: At any point during the workshop you call out 'STOP'. No matter what is going on, everyone stops and faces you. • Having everyone's attention, you now tell the group a brief statement, e.g. 'I was so clever at organising the serious things at work that I am now free to enjoy today's fun activities' • Here's the ask: 'Because of that I want a standing ovation!' • All the workshop participants stand, and facing the person, give a wild standing ovation – making eye contact, smiling, clapping and cheering. • When the standing ovation is done, the workshop resumes.
Benefits:	Builds relationship in a group
Safety, Risks or Difficulties:	This exercise can be difficult for shy people.
Limits:	
Adaptations:	Standing ovations can be extended to other than workshop situations e.g. during staff meetings.

Other considerations:	This activity makes noise. No one is forced to ask for a standing ovation. This activity can also be done with children and adolescents.
Variations:	• The group can join together (pre-emptively) to extend the standing ovation to a new (unsuspecting) person entering the group.

24 These Are My Hands

Who:	Any Group
Number of players:	2+
Ages:	Adolescents, Adults, Seniors
Equipment:	
Duration:	Short to Medium Play
Where:	Anywhere
When:	Any time
How:	• The group moves around the space greeting one another. • The leader gives a signal for the participants to stop and examine the hands of the person they are standing with. • Describe the things you notice about one another's hands (rings, scars, freckles, etc.) • Continue the games meeting new people and examining their hands. Once the leader feels the group has met with enough people they can ask the group to sit down in a circle and discuss as a group.
Benefits:	Memory, Rapport Building, Communication, Sensitivity
Safety, Risks or Difficulties:	
Limits:	
Adaptations:	Can be adapted for older children (Age 6+)
	• Participants approach quietly and silently place their hands on the volunteer who tries to guess if the hands they are touching are male or female
Other considerations:	The exercise can help participants to recall past experiences and reflect on different times in their lives. It is an outlet to share one's story and feel they are being heard.
Variations:	*Male / Female*[2] A volunteer sits on a chair wearing a blindfold (or with eyes closed), with their hands resting on their knees palms up.

25 Changing Chairs

Who:	Any Group
Number of players:	8+
Ages:	Any Age
Equipment:	Chairs – one fewer than the number of people in the group
Duration:	Short to Medium Play, depending on group size
Where:	Open space that will accommodate all the chairs to be set up in a large circle.
When:	Good introductory activity, but can also be used at any time.
How:	• Everyone sitting on a chair in a circle with one person in the middle • People, by simple eye contact, attempt to change seats before person in centre can capture a chair
Benefits:	Ice Breaker, Stress Reduction, Physical
Safety, Risks or Difficulties:	Can be fast paced and in a small space there is the potential for people to trip or fall
Limits:	Not suitable for people who use wheelchairs or who have significant physical or visual restrictions
Adaptations:	
Other considerations:	
Variations:	Several variations on this game can be found in Warren, B. (2011) *Drama Games (Revisited)* Captus Press, North York, on e.g. • *Will you change places with me?* (p.71) • *Master and Slave*

26 Frau Holler Ist Krank

Who:	Any Group
Number of players:	6+
Ages:	Any Age
Equipment:	Chairs an asset but not essential
Duration:	Short to Medium Play (depending on the size of the group)
Where:	Any space that accommodates the circle.
When:	At any time
How:	• Mrs. Holler is ill • Played in a circle • An accumulation game with actions • As you go round, each person says 'Mrs. Holler is ill she has . . .' and then names an illness e.g.: ○ 'an eye ache' (person then does action – rubbing eyes) • Everybody copies the action Then moves on to the next person who might say 'Mrs. Holler is ill she has eye-ache and a sore nose . . .' and so on all the way around the circle with each person adding a new illness / disease.
Benefits:	Group Building, Physical, Imagination, Memory
Safety, Risks or Difficulties:	May pose some problems for people with memory problems
Limits:	Not suitable for people who use wheelchairs or who have significant physical or visual restrictions
Adaptations:	
Other considerations:	
Variations:	

27 Love Heart Tennis

Who:	Anyone /Any Group
Number of players:	6
Ages:	Adolescents, Adults, Seniors
Equipment:	4 x soft plastic fly swatters, 1 roll of 2 ply toilet paper and 6 chairs and a balloon
Duration:	Short to Medium Play
Where:	Activity / Common Room
When:	Any time but works best in the middle of a session
How:	• This mimics a doubles game of tennis. There are 4 players comprising 2 players on each side facing each other. 2 people holding the toilet paper make the net. A 'Love Heart Balloon' is blown up and tied off. This is the 'tennis ball'. A game of 'Love Heart Tennis' can now be played. Normal tennis rules can be applied. Best out of 3 or 5 also works.
Benefits:	Physical, Group Building, Stress Reduction
Safety, Risks or Difficulties:	This exercise can be so exciting that it is possible to fall out of the chair!

Figure 6.3 Love Heart Tennis

	Sufficient separation between plays to prevent hitting each other.
Limits:	Requires good hand / eye co-ordination.
Adaptations:	Family can join in. This can become a daily or weekly event. Can be played from a wheelchair.
Other considerations:	Energy raising exercise. Builds team-work. Great photo opportunity.
Variations:	• Staff can play 'against' each other. • Residents can play 'against' each other. • A staff member can join with a resident. • Management staff can also join in.

28 Jelly Belly (Ha Ha Ha)

Who:	Any Group
Number of players:	10+
Ages:	Adolescents, Adults
Equipment:	
Duration:	Medium Play
Where:	Activity room with a clean floor, preferably carpeted
When:	Near the end of group activity.
How:	• All participants lie on their back, on the floor one at a time so that: ◦ #2's head is on #1's stomach, ◦ #3's head is on #2's stomach and so on until all are on the floor – The overall effect being a herringbone pattern • Every participant except the first and last, will have their head on another's person's stomach and someone's head on their stomach ◦ #1 then says Ha, ◦ #2 says Ha, ha, ◦ #3 Ha, ha, ha, and so on down the line. • When the game works, all the players are laughing uproariously before the end.
Benefits:	Group Building, Stress Reduction, Physical, Sensitivity, Communication
Safety, Risks or Difficulties:	May be problematic for people who are 'touch phobic' or from ethnic groups with prohibitions on physical touching between sexes
Limits:	
Adaptations:	Can be adapted to include other age groups – children and seniors
Other considerations:	
Variations:	While lying on the floor, one at a time, each person tries to tell a joke

29 Massage Train

Who:	Any Group
Number of players:	Groups of 6+
Ages:	Adolescents and Adults
Equipment:	
Duration:	Short Play
Where:	Any space that accommodates a circle of six or more
When:	• Can work well at the beginning, middle or end of any group activity. • This is a quick activity that energises the group. • Used at the beginning, this is an icebreaker. • Used at the middle, this is a positive break. At the end, it continues to connect the group.
How:	• Participants stand to form a circle with arms almost touching. • Everyone turns to their right. • Begin massaging the trapezius of the person in front. • Making noise is an integral and important part of the exercise.

Figure 6.4 Massage Train

	• Noises like: 'Oh yes. . .', 'That feels good. . .', 'Don't stop. . .', 'Harder, harder. . .' After 1–2 minutes everyone turns to the left and repeats the procedure for a further 1–2 minutes.
Benefits:	Ice Breaker, Group Building, Stress Reduction
Safety, Risks or Difficulties:	May be problematic for people who are 'touch phobic' or from ethnic groups with prohibitions on physical touching between sexes People must be comfortable being touched and massaged. Anyone with significant upper back problems, or a boil, can still enjoy watching the activity.
Limits:	Requires good balance and ability to raise and use arms. Not for use at bedside
Adaptations:	Can be adapted for wheelchairs or seated groups with appropriate angling of chairs With more than 20 people, you may want to consider more than one massage circle.
Other considerations:	How well does the group know one another? As long as the group knows one another this works very well at the beginning of a session. However for a group that has just met it may be better to wait until later. Presents possibilities for good photo opportunity in professional workshop settings.
Variations:	

30 My Favourite Tunes . . . (a Variation on 'Desert Island Discs')

Who:	Any Group
Number of players:	4+
Ages:	Adolescents, Adults, Seniors
Equipment:	Chairs are useful but not essential
Duration:	Short to Medium Play
Where:	Any space that will accommodate a circle.
When:	Anytime

How:	• This activity is done in a group.
	• Leader explains that each person is to be cast away on a desert island. They may take with them 8 tunes.
	• Each person is asked to list the tunes they wish to take and share their list with the group explaining why they chose each tune/song
	  ◦ Participants can be asked to:
	    – share all eight at once or one song at a time

Benefits:	Communication, Sensitivity, Rapport Building, Memory
Safety, Risks or Difficulties:	May cause some people to become tearful or sad.
Limits:	

Adaptations:	With groups of more than 12 can be played in pairs.
	  ◦ pairs take turns actively listening to each other's list.
	  ◦ When both are finished they rejoin the group and share all or part of their discussion

Other considerations:	This exercise provides participants the opportunity to exercise 'active listening' and patience.

Variations:	• When / where appropriate
	  ◦ A discussion can be held concerning: musical choices and / or
	  ◦ what it would be like to be shipwrecked on a desert island
	• Participants can also be asked to list other items to take with e.g.:
	  ◦ One book
	  ◦ One luxury item

31 Song Circle

Who:	Any Group
Number of players:	5+
Ages:	Adolescents, Adults, Seniors
Equipment:	
Duration:	Short to Medium Play
Where:	Anywhere.
When:	Can work well at any point in group activity.

How:	• Participants stand in a circle facing each other
	• Leader begins by singing a song or short phrase (verse or chorus) from any song
	    ◦ All other participants are encouraged to either
	        – Join in (if they know the song), or
	        – Hum along (if they don't)
	• Then going around the circle each participant leads the song circle
	• This can continue for as long or as short as needed
	    ◦ Length of time will be related to number of people in the group.

Benefits:	Ice Breaker, Memory, Group Building, Stress Reduction, Physical
Safety, Risks or Difficulties:	Some people feel awkward about singing in public
Limits:	
Adaptations:	Can be adapted for wheelchairs or seated groups with appropriate angling of chairs
Other considerations:	Can get very noisy. Watch for smiles and facial expression changes.

Variations:	• Participants can be asked to sing songs around a theme:
	    ◦ Love Songs, Children's songs, Drinking songs etc.
	    ◦ Alphabet / Numbers – Songs must begin with the letter A or B or C etc. or include a number in the title
	• Discussion with participants re: their memories of the songs sung

32 Juggling Tunes

Who:	Any Group
Number of players:	5+
Ages:	Adolescents, Adults
Equipment:	Juggling balls or bean bags
Duration:	Short to Medium Play
Where:	Activity / Common Room
When:	Can work well at any point in group activity
How:	• Stand in a circle facing inwards, leader begins singing a simple song that everyone is familiar with: e.g. 'You Are my Sunshine' • All participants are encouraged to join in. • Leader then introduces a juggling ball (bean bag) and asks each member of the group to throw the ball to someone else in the circle. • This is repeated so that the ball always passes around the circle in EXACTLY THE SAME PATTERN e.g. from Peter to Bernie to Suzie to Alf to June to Azra to Amber to Peter to Bernie etc. . . • Once pattern has been repeated a couple of times the group then resumes singing : 'You Are my Sunshine' while throwing the ball in the established pattern
Benefits:	Communication, Group Building, Stress Reduction, Physical
Safety, Risks or Difficulties:	Difficulty – some people feel awkward about singing in public
Limits:	Requires good physical dexterity and hand / eye coordination Not suitable for people with severe physical or visual limitations
Adaptations:	Can be adapted for wheelchairs or seated groups with appropriate angling of chairs
Other considerations:	Can get very noisy. Watch for smiles and facial expression changes
Variations:	• Introduce additional juggling balls (up to # of people in group)

	• Have participants move around the room (walk, run, skip) while singing and throwing the ball in the established pattern • Change the song being sung and have the group move to the rhythm of the song

33 Stump the Chump

Who:	Any Group
Number of players:	Can be played in pairs, in a circle of 5+, or in two teams as a competition
Ages:	Any Age
Equipment:	
Duration:	Short to Medium Play
Where:	Any space
	• Can be played at bedside
When:	• Works best after *Song Circle* (p.71)
	BUT Can work well at any point
How:	**In pairs** • One person says a word, ANY word (e.g. 'Green' or 'River', 'Toothbrush' etc.), and challenges the other to sing a song that includes that particular word • Each person takes it in turns to challenge the other **In a circle** As for work in pairs BUT the person saying the word challenges the person on their left to sing the song associated with the word.
Benefits:	Ice Breaker, Imagination, Group Building, Stress Reduction, Physical
Safety, Risks or Difficulties:	Difficulty – some people feel awkward about singing in public
Limits:	At the bedside be aware of others in the room
Adaptations:	Can be adapted for wheelchairs or seated groups with appropriate angling of chairs
Other considerations:	Can get very noisy. Watch for smiles and facial expression changes.

Variations:	• Participants can be asked to sing a song:
	  ◦ That begins or ends with the word.
	  ◦ Make up a song about the word
	• Can be played in 2 teams as a competition – each team scoring a point when:
	  ◦ they successfully sing a song about the word
	  ◦ or conversely, when the word 'Stumps' the other team

34 Cats and Dogs

Who:	Anyone/Any Group
Number of players:	2+
Ages:	Any Age
Equipment:	
Duration:	Short Play
Where:	Any space
When:	• Can be a good warm up for *Song Circle* (p.71) BUT Can work well at any point
How:	Played in pairs, or in small teams • First pairs sing a well known, easy to sing song e.g. 'You Are my Sunshine' • Then they sing the same song by singing the tune like dogs i.e. substituting 'woof' or 'barking' (or similar) for the words • Next they repeat this process only now singing the tune like cats i.e. substituting 'miaow' or 'purring' (or similar) for the words Lastly they sing a 'duet' with one partner singing like a dog the other like a cat.
Benefits:	Ice Breaker, Communication, Imagination, Group Building, Stress Reduction, Physical
Safety, Risks or Difficulties:	Difficulty – some people feel awkward about singing in public
Limits:	Can be adapted for wheelchairs or seated groups with appropriate angling of chairs
Adaptations:	
Other considerations:	Usually gets very noisy. Watch for smiles and facial expression changes.
Variations:	• Can repeat process using: ◦ Different songs ◦ Singing as different animals

35 Look, Hold, Become

Who:	Any Group
Number of players:	4+
Ages:	Any Age
Equipment:	
Duration:	Medium to Long Play
Where:	Activity / Common Room
When:	Can work well at any point but preferably after a few warm up activities.
How:	• 3 stages and 3 commands • Participants spread out around the room. • Stage 1: leaders asks participants to look around the room at different objects (chairs, wall, floor tile, etc.) Humorous requests such as looking at your nose, back of your head, etc. are welcome as long as it is clear they are meant for humour. • Stage 2: players pretend to hold objects • Examples for commands: Imagine you are holding a furry cat in your hands; Imagine you are holding an ice cream; or Imagine you are holding a bowl brim-full of water. • The leader should provide examples by doing the commands themselves • Stage 3: become something else. Examples: Become a tree or become the letter C, become a firefighter
Benefits:	Imagination, Physical
Safety, Risks or Difficulties:	
Limits:	With a smaller group participants might feel they are more in the spotlight and less comfortable to allow themselves to be fully immersed in the activity.
Adaptations:	
Other considerations:	This activity allows participants to loosen up and feel comfortable in their own bodies and with their fellow participants.
Variations:	

36 What Are You Doing (mime)?

Who:	Any Group
Number of players:	5+
Ages:	Any Age
Equipment:	
Duration:	Short to Medium Play
Where:	Any space that accommodates the circle
When:	Can work well at any point in group activity

How:	• Participants stand in a circle facing inwards
	• Leader mimes an action e.g. Shaving
	• Person on left (Participant #1) ask the 'What are you doing?'
	• Leader replies with anything but what s/he is miming!
	  ◦ E.g. 'Shampooing my goldfish' or 'Milking a tiger'
	• #1 now has to mime this action
	• #2 in circle now asks #1 'What are you doing?'
	• #1's response is ANYTHING but what they are miming and #2 has to mime this new 'lie'
	• This continues around the circle until everyone has mimed an action
	• This can continue for as long or as short as needed
	  ◦ Length of time will be related to number of people in the group.

Benefits:	Ice Breaker, Group Building, Stress Reduction, Imagination
Safety, Risks or Difficulties:	
Limits:	
Adaptations:	Can be played seated to accommodate people who use wheelchairs
Other considerations:	Can get very noisy. Watch for smiles and facial expression changes.
Variations:	• Once one revolution of the circle is complete the process in reverse direction

37 Sound Volley Ball

Who:	Any Group
Number of players:	2+
Ages:	Adolescents, Adults
Equipment:	
Duration:	Short to Medium Play
Where:	Activity / Common Room (can be played outdoors)
When:	Consider this early to middle of group activity.
How:	• The game is played like volleyball but players ◦ use an 'imaginary ball' whose trajectory is created by body movement, eye contact and vocal sound ◦ may be played in pairs or small teams. • Teams stand facing each other. • Server makes eye contact with a player on the other team • They serve the ball while saying an elongated vowel e.g. OOOO or AAAAH or EEEEE • The receiver of the 'ball' must hit it to one of the other team's players before it hits the ground (the sound stops)
Benefits:	Physical, Imagination, Communication, Group Building
Safety, Risks or Difficulties:	Make sure there is enough rooms between teams to avoid physical contact • Room needs to be cleared of tables and chairs
Limits:	Not suitable for people who use wheelchairs or who have significant physical restrictions
Adaptations:	• Can be played seated as 'Table Tennis' • Can be played competitively with each team getting a point if the ball is 'dropped' • The rules of Volley Ball can be adapted to the needs of the group.
Other considerations:	
Variations:	• Use a real volley ball net • Instead of vowels, use; ◦ Names ◦ Sounds e.g. 'Boing' • Create stories – one word at time

38 Imaginary Ball Toss (Whoosh, Whaa, Bugga Bugga. . .)

Who:	Any Group
Number of players:	Groups of 8+
Ages:	Adolescents, Adults, Seniors
Equipment:	
Duration:	Medium Play
Where:	Common / Activity Room
When:	Can work well at almost any point in group activity.
How:	• A circle is formed. • The leader passes an imaginary ball (IB) to the person on their right while making the sound 'WHOOSH'. The ball is passed from person to person around the circle with every pass being accompanied by a WHOOSH. • Variations: a. At any point as the IB is being passed to them, the intended receiver (IR) can suddenly raise both arms in the air with hands open exclaiming – WHAA! This is a way of saying that the ball will not be accepted. So the original thrower has no option but to pass the ball in the other direction. i. This action can be done at any time and by Anyone. So, now at any point a person can WHOOSH or WHAA. b. As the IB arrives, the IR can extend their arms horizontally with palms touching and point to any other person in the circle (except their neighbour) and passing the imaginary ball with the sound of ZAP. i. The person being ZAPPED now has a choice of a WHOOSH, a WHAA or a ZAP. c. As the IB arrives, player says 'BOING' while holding arms over the head with palm together pointing skywards, whilst at the same time bending the knees. Everyone in the circle follows copies and says 'BOING' in unison – When this is done, the ball can be passed on with a WHOOSH, WHAA or a ZAP d. If at any point a mistake is made, any person can start jumping from leg to leg, saying BUGGA. . .

	BUGGA. . .BUGGA with everyone following suit. When this is done, the ball can be passed on.
Benefits:	Ice Breaker, Communication, Group Building, Stress Reduction, Physical
Safety, Risks or Difficulties:	Some people may be uncomfortable saying 'Bugga'.
Limits:	Requires good balance and ability to raise and use arms. Not for use at bedside Certain elements may present challenges for people with limited mobility
Adaptations:	Can be adapted for wheelchairs or seated groups with appropriate angling of chairs
Other considerations:	How well does the group know one another? As long as the group knows one another this works very well at the beginning of a session. However for a group a group that has just met it may be better to wait until later.
Variations:	• Can be used at the end of the day to energise the group.

39 Stupid Magic

Who:	Anyone / Any Group
Number of players:	Any Number
Ages:	Any Age
Equipment:	
Duration:	Short Play
Where:	Anywhere
When:	At any time
How:	• Tell the group that you have amazing magic and you are going to make everyone disappear. • Tell everyone they must do exactly as they are told for the magic to work • Tell them to count to three out loud • On 'Three' in a theatrical fashion say a magic word . . . e.g. Abracadabra and • Theatrically close YOUR Eyes proclaiming. . . OMG Everyone has disappeared . . . It's MAGIC!! Then make an equally theatrical show of having everyone count to three again . . . say the magic word again and open eyes
Benefits:	Communication, Rapport, Diversionary
Safety, Risks or Difficulties:	As usual with 'magic' plays, practice is important.
Limits:	
Adaptations:	Can be used in family / social settings
Other considerations:	Can be used at the bedside or as a diversion in a treatment room
Variations:	• Tell everyone that you have magic that allows you to make yourself invisible • This time, using the same theatricality, ask the group to close THEIR eyes • As soon as they have closed their eyes say 'See, now I am INVISIBLE'

40 Squeaky Magic

Who:	Any Group
Number of players:	Any Number
Ages:	Any Age
Equipment:	Small hand held squeaker(s)
Duration:	Short Play
Where:	Anywhere
When:	At any time
How:	• Place a small squeaker in your hand. • Make sure this is hidden from view. • Touch your nose and press on squeaker • Touch another part of your body e.g. your belly button and repeat Watch faces (young and young at heart) light up with smiles!
Benefits:	Rapport, Diversionary, Communication
Safety, Risks or Difficulties:	As usual with 'magic' plays, practice is important. TIMING is very important You need to practice using the squeaker so that you time touching an object or body part at the same time as you press on the squeaker!
Limits:	At bedside be aware of others in the room
Adaptations:	Can be used in family / social settings
Other considerations:	• There are many sounds a squeaker can make e.g. the sound of a horn or siren • Also there are squeakers that you can place in your mouth e.g.: ○ You can take the squeaker out of a dog's chew toy and use this way
Variations:	• You can make ANYTHING squeak – floors, walls, TV sets et. . . • You can magically remove the squeak with a magic word e.g. Abracadabra or 'smelly socks' • You can place squeakers in your shoes, waistband, bra (women) or underwear

41 Magic Newspaper

Who:	Any Group
Number of players:	5+
Ages:	Adolescents, Adults
Equipment:	A daily newspaper; chairs are an asset.
Duration:	Medium Play
Where:	Anywhere
When:	Can work well at any point

How:	• Participants sit in a circle facing inwards
	• Leader tells the group that the newspaper is *magic.*
	• Leader transforms the newspaper saying 'Before your very eyes I will magically transform this newspaper' . . . 'as soon as you know what it has become call out so everyone knows'
	• The newspaper can be
	  ◦ made into a *hat*;
	  ◦ used as a *cricket* or *baseball bat*;
	  ◦ part of a mimed scene e.g. *drinking beer in a pub where the newspaper is the handle for pouring the beer*[3]
	• As soon as the group identifies what the newspaper has become . . . you can exclaim . . . 'Bloody Magic' . . . 'works every time. . .' (or something similar)
	• Then the newspaper is passed around the circle with each participant creating something with it.
	  ◦ The only limits to what can be created with the newspaper are the imaginations of the group
	• This can continue for as long or as short as needed Length of time will be related to number of people in the group.

Benefits:	Imagination, Ice Breaker, Group Building, Stress Reduction
Safety, Risks or Difficulties:	Some people *freeze* when first confronted with the newspaper
Limits:	

Adaptations:	Can be adapted for older children and for Seniors but for people with fine motor skill problems there may be some difficulty manipulating the newspaper.
Other considerations:	
Variations:	All transformations thematic e.g. clothing or musical instruments

42 Tape Measure Telephone

Who:	Anyone / Any Group
Number of players:	1+
Ages:	Any Age
Equipment:	Small metal tape measure
Duration:	Short Play
Where:	Anywhere
When:	At any time

Figure 6.5 Tape Measure Telephone

How:	• This is an 'Ambush of the Intellect' play. • A tape measure is constantly available – in the pocket, in the bag, in the Humour Cart etc • When anyone's cell phone rings, quickly pick up your tape measure. • Extend the tape to about 1 foot and hold in this position. • Bring the tape measure to the ear and begin any imaginary conversation. • A short time into the conversation make note that the signal is beginning to fade. • Now extend the tape even further to improve the signal and then continue the imaginary conversation. • Finish the conversation politely noting that you are in the middle of a workshop. Press on the tape release button to quickly retract the tape. Put the tape measure away as if nothing has happened.
Benefits:	Diversionary, Communication, Imagination
Safety, Risks or Difficulties:	Timing is VERY important
Limits:	
Adaptations:	Can be used in supermarkets, on buses, at airports etc
Other considerations:	This is a piece of improv. Important to keep a straight face.
Variations:	• Can pass the tape measure to partner / friend to continue the play • The tape measure can be replaced with a banana

43 Floating Cup Magic

Who:	Anyone / Any Group
	Patients / Clients / Residents
Number of players:	One on one
Ages:	Children
Equipment:	Styrofoam or paper (preferred) cup
Duration:	Short Play
Where:	Consulting room (possible at bedside)
When:	• At any point in the consultation
How:	• Practitioner shows the patient that with concentration, a cup initially held in both hands can be made to float. • Once the float is performed, the technique is shown and patient now shows the practitioner the float. • A thumb is inserted through the cup, which is cradled and supported between both hands. The cup is held is such a way that the audience doesn't see inside it. • With some magic words and concentration, the hands are very slowly separated and the cup seemingly can be floated about. At the end of the play, the hands grasp the cup, which is then put away.
Benefits:	Communication, Rapport Builder, Diversionary
Safety, Risks or Difficulties:	As usual with 'magic' plays, practice is important.
Limits:	
Adaptations:	Can be used in family / social settings
Other considerations:	At one level this is a mentor – apprentice relationship. Passing on 'trade secrets' is a linking activity. Patient is learning performance skills.
Variations:	

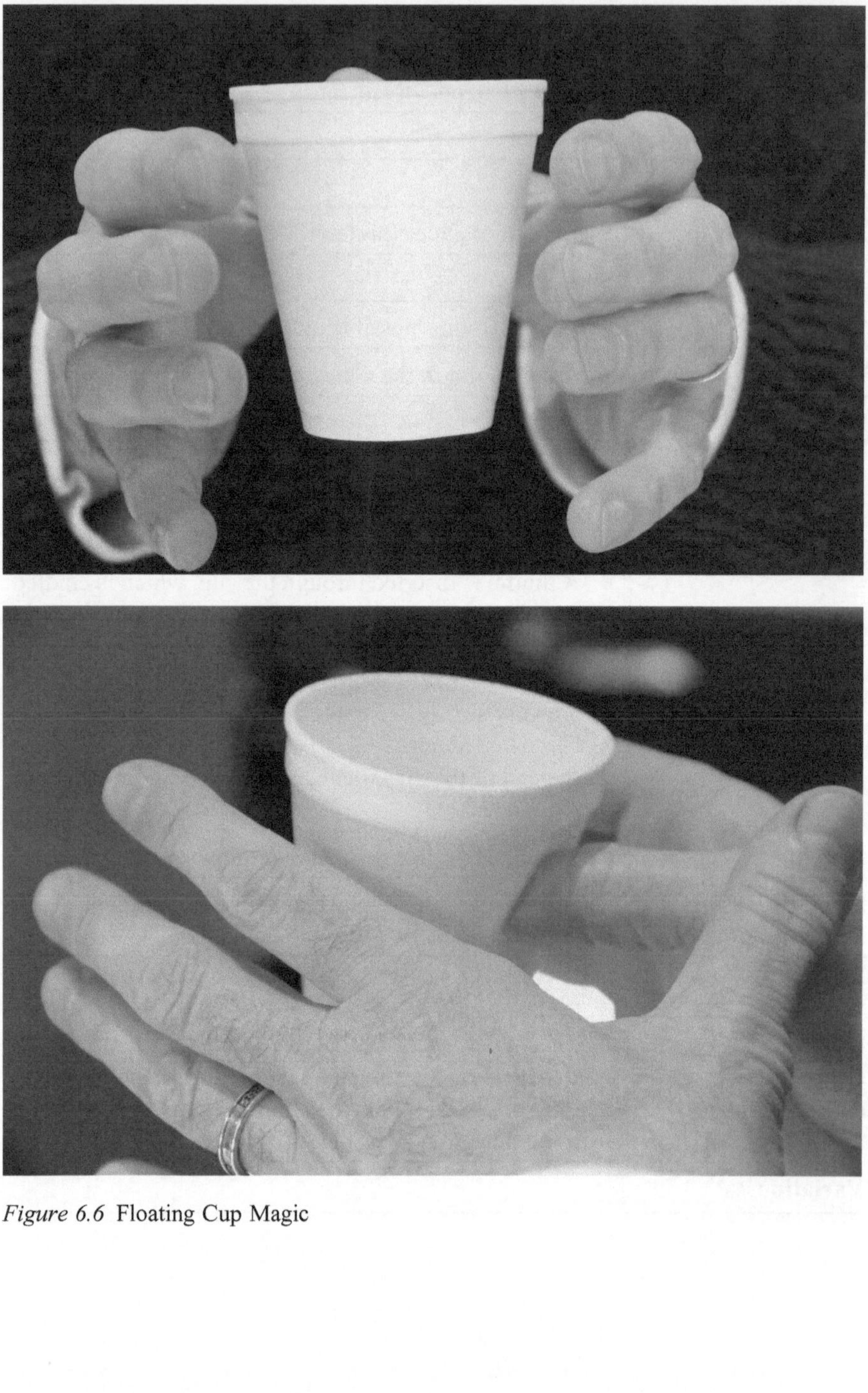

Figure 6.6 Floating Cup Magic

44 Imp Bottle

Who:	Anyone / Any Group
	Patients / Clients
Number of players:	Individual
Ages:	Any Age
Equipment:	Imp Bottle
Duration:	Short Play
Where:	Anywhere
When:	At any point in the consultation
How:	• Bring out the Imp Bottle and show that it only ever does 2 things – stand up and lie down. That's it and that's all it ever does. • In this close-up play, hand over the Imp Bottle and invite your observer to lay it down horizontally. No way! They can stand it up but they can't lie it down. • Take back the Imp Bottle and show how easily it can stand up as well as lie down. • Give the observer one more attempt and again, they can't lie it down. • This play relies on changes in the centre of gravity by secretly removing a small metal rod from the shaft of the Imp Bottle. Examples are shown on YouTube.
Benefits:	Ice Breaker, Rapport Builder, Communication, Diversionary, Physical
Safety, Risks or Difficulties:	As usual with 'magic' plays, practice is important.
Limits:	
Adaptations:	Play can start in one room and be continued into other spaces.
Other considerations:	Better on a smooth horizontal surface. Practice 're-loading' the Imp Bottle without giving the game away.
Variations:	

45 Magic Colouring Book

Who:	Anyone / Any Group
	Patients / Clients
Number of players:	1+, Individual + onlookers
Ages:	Children
Equipment:	Magic colouring book
Duration:	Short Play
Where:	Consulting room
When:	At any time
How:	• Lead into discussion about drawing and pencils then ask if they colour in books. • Whatever the answer, disclose that you really, really enjoy colouring in. • A technical issue is a discussion about whether or not one 'crosses the line' • Tell them that you are so careful not to cross over the line that it took you 4 months (holding up only 3 fingers) to do the work. Usually they will correct you here. • Reach out for the books in the book shelf and show them the cover. Talk about being so proud of excellent work. Hold the book by its spine and from the BOTTOM edge flip the pages over (keeping eye contact with the patient) The pages are all blank. They will react. Having realised the 'work' has disappeared ask for their help to find the work. They help by softly and very gently touching an open hand on the cover. • This time flip the pages from the TOP edge. Every page now has a black drawing outline. Someone will notice there are no colours! • Again, ask for help to find the colours. This can be done by using a fingertip to tap on the different colours on the cover. • Now flip the pages from the MIDDLE of the book and every page will now have a colour drawing. • 'Magic Coloring Book' on YouTube gives visual instructions.

Benefits:	Rapport Builder, Communication, Stress Reduction, Diversionary
Safety, Risks or Difficulties:	
Limits:	
Adaptations:	Can also be used in family setting. Others can also help finding the colours. At subsequent consultations, the child can guess the content of the book – i.e. blank, black and white or colour. They will be correct 100% of the time.
Other considerations:	
Variations:	The child can also use a magic wand.

46 D'Lite

Who:	Anyone / Any Group
Number of players:	1+
Ages:	All Ages
Equipment:	D'lite latex thumb tip
Duration:	Short Play
Where:	Anywhere (better indoors)
When:	Anytime there's a need for surprise or distraction
How:	• The D'lite is a battery / light containing lightweight thumb tip • Easily carried in a pocket or purse or kept in a draw. • Slip on the D'lite over the thumb. • Keeping the hand moving will reduce detection of the D'lite. • Pressing the thumb and forefinger activates a red light at the thumb tip. Letting go of the pressure switches off the light. • The D'lite can be used to pick up any 'hot spots' anywhere and 'disappear' them. D'lite on YouTube gives visual cues.
Benefits:	Diversionary, Ice Breaker, Rapport Builder, Communication
Safety, Risks or Difficulties:	Main difficulty is getting the timing right – practice on your family or staff
Limits:	Not as clear in day light
Adaptations:	Can be used during presentations, in the car, at the restaurant etc.
Other considerations:	Amazing surprise. Quick distraction.
Variations:	Use to get heat out of the ear, throat, burn etc

47 Disappearing Silk

Who:	Anyone / Any Group
Number of players:	2+
Ages:	Any Age
Equipment:	Small square colourful piece of silk eg 10cm square. A latex / plastic thumb stall.
Duration:	Short Play
Where:	Anywhere
When:	Anytime
How:	• A silk is shown. It can be dangled over a sore part; it can sweep the air; it can be sneezed onto. • The silk is held in one hand then gently squeezed and pushed into the opposite, loosely closed hand. It is shown slowly disappearing into the hand until completely gone. • A magic word such as abracadabra, or a special pass is made over the hand. • The hands are separated and the silk has completely vanished. • At some point later, there is the option of making the silk re-appear from behind the ear, or pocket or from a book etc • See YouTube for visual instructions.
Benefits:	Communication, Stress Reduction, Diversionary,
Safety, Risks or Difficulties:	Difficulty is in the timing.
Limits:	Best in close-up.
Adaptations:	Easily adapted to procedures (before gloving up) The silk can be given away
Other considerations:	
Variations:	Unlimited. Patient can help the silk to disappear.

48 Glove Balloon

Who:	Any Group
Number of players:	1 with onlookers.
Ages:	Children.
Equipment:	Large latex glove
Duration:	Short Play
Where:	Consulting room usually. Also works with small audience (take plenty of gloves!!)
When:	Anytime – best at end of consultation – a time for brief play

Figure 6.7 Glove Balloon

How:	• A large, soft latex glove is blown up to the size of a large hand. • The end is twisted to avoid air loss and is then stretched and a simple knot made. • The fore and middle fingers are crossed. The ring and little fingers are crossed. • After a moment or two the fingers will fill with air and now the hand puppet can stand on its own. • Eyes and a smile can be easily drawn to add to the caricature. The glove balloon is offered to the child.
Benefits:	Ice Breaker, Rapport Builder, Stress Reduction, Diversionary, Physical
Safety, Risks or Difficulties:	Exclude latex allergy
Limits:	Will become very busy if several children are present. They'll all want one!
Adaptations:	The child can show how the balloon sneezes to a parent or sibling
Other considerations:	If the child doesn't accept the glove balloon from you, they will usually take it from the parent.
Variations:	Before crossing the fingers hold the end and the middle fingers. Stretch and a shark will magically appear

49 Magic Tongue Depressor

Who:	Anyone / Any Group
	Patient / Client
Number of players:	1 with onlookers.
Ages:	Children
Equipment:	Wooden tongue depressor
Duration:	Short Play
Where:	Anywhere
When:	Anytime.
How:	• Wooden tongue depressor is best. Write child's name in bold on one side before they enter the room. • Leave with name face down. • Pick up tongue depressor and show the blank side. • Use the Paddle Move to show the other side is also blank – ie both sides are blank. The Paddle Move combines a turn with a twist so that only the one (blank) side is being shown although; done quickly it looks like both sides are being shown. • The child can say a special/magic word and suddenly their name appears. Not only on one side but also on the other side. It can also completely disappear and reappear. • This can be taught to an older child (over 10) • Paddle Move tutorials are available on YouTube
Benefits:	Ice Breaker, Rapport Builder, Communication, Stress Reduction, Diversionary, Physical
Safety, Risks or Difficulties:	Practice in the Paddle Move is needed here – best in front of a mirror first.
Limits:	
Adaptations:	Also consider as part of ENT exam
Other considerations:	
Variations:	Practice on staff can be fun

50 Sponge Ball Magic

Who:	Anyone / Any Group
Number of players:	1 with onlookers
Ages:	Any Age – especially children.
Equipment:	4 x 1 inch sponge balls
Duration:	Short Play
Where:	Anywhere
When:	Anytime
How:	• Show 3 sponge balls in the palm of the left hand • One sponge ball is hidden in the right hand with 3 / 4 / 5 fingers slightly flexed • Ask patient to keep open their hand palm upwards and help with counting. With the right hand pick up one of the 3 balls and place it in their hand. Ask – how many balls in your hand? Pick up that ball and return to your open left hand. • Now pick up 2 balls and place in patient's hand. Ask how many do you have now? • Pick up the 2 balls and return to your open left hand. • Do the same using the 3 balls and return them to your left hand. • Next, pick up one ball and place on patient's hand having slipped the hidden ball as well. That is, 2 sponge balls squashed together are placed in the patient's hand and immediately help them close the fingers tight asking them to make sure the hand is kept close. • You are left with 2 balls in your left hand. Pick one up and show putting it in pocket. • Now it seems that they hold one ball, one ball is in the open left hand and one is in your pocket. • Now with the click of the right hand 'make' the ball in the pocket fly through the air into the patient's closed hand. • Ask the patient to open their hand to reveal 2 balls. Sponge Ball Magic instructions available on YouTube.
Benefits:	Ice Breaker, Rapport Builder, Reframing, Communication, Stress Reduction, Diversionary

Safety, Risks or Difficulties:	Practice makes perfect.
Limits:	
Adaptations:	
Other considerations:	
Variations:	This play is one-on-one. Active onlookers also enjoy the play.

51 Finger Puppets

Who:	Patients / Clients
Number of players:	Usually one-on-one. BUT can be 'performed' with a larger audience.
Ages:	Children
Equipment:	Small finger puppet
Duration:	Short Play
Where:	Anywhere but works particularly well at the bedside or in consulting room
When:	At any time
How:	• A finger puppet is fitted on a finger – typically the forefinger of the right hand. • The left arm is raised to the horizontal position. This will represent the stage. • The finger puppet is slowly raised about the stage height. The finger puppet can talk, tell a story, sing a song or engage in dialogue with the patient.
Benefits:	Diversionary, Builds Rapport, Communication
Safety, Risks or Difficulties:	As usual with 'magic' plays, practice is important. *Practice in front of a mirror.*
Limits:	
Adaptations:	Can be used in family/social settings – in fact any setting with children present. Can also be used with adults and seniors. However hand puppets probably a better bet. Can work VERY well as a diversion during minor invasive procedures
Other considerations:	This exercise is suitable for any close up play with children. Puppets are a rich source of imagination. Good way to initiate play and story telling.

Variations:	Finger puppet eyes are very effective. • Give a finger puppet to the child. ◦ Allow the child to lead the adult. • Use hand puppets – especially animals with adults and seniors

52 Humour Cart

Who:	Anyone / Any Group
Number of players:	Any Number
Ages:	Any Age
Equipment:	2 level Stainless Steel Cart – or similar
Duration:	Spontaneous
Where:	Anywhere. (Best in any healthcare setting including clinic or residential facility)
When:	At any time
How:	• Drug trolleys deliver medicines. A humour cart delivers play and fun. • Any stainless steel/wooden cart can be transformed into a magical animal or structure using a variety of materials. • Adding props to the Humour Cart is a lot of fun. Props can be added over time. Props can include puppets, magic plays eg the Imp Bottle, toys etc • Some props can sit on the structure whilst other props can be 'hidden' in a draw (if there is one). • Once prepared, the Humour Cart will develop a character of its own – as it settles into the role of a mobile play centre.
Benefits:	Communication, Rapport Builder, Imagination
Safety, Risks or Difficulties:	
Limits:	
Adaptations:	Can be used with family also.
Other considerations:	• This structure invites fun and play from other staff. • The Humour Cart can be a part of the healthcare environmental setting – ready to play at any time.
Variations:	Other staff members can trigger play using the Humour Cart at any time.

53 Humour Yourself

Who:	Professionals / Staff
Number of players:	Best with 9+
Ages:	Adult
Equipment:	Paper+Pencil
Duration:	10–15 minutes
Where:	Anywhere

How:	• Form groups of 3. One person is the scribe.
	• Divide an A4 page into 3 columns with the following headings:
	• HUMOUR YOURSELF: HUMOUR YOUR STAFF: HUMOUR YOUR PATIENTS/CLIENTS
	• There is no right or wrong answer. No names are used.
	• The group works together to stretch their collective imagination to write:
	  ○ What are the possible plays / activities that can be used to HUMOUR YOURSELF.
	  ○ What are the possible plays / activities that can be used to engage with and HUMOUR YOUR STAFF.
	  ○ What are the possible plays/activities that can be used to engage and interact with YOUR RESIDENTS / CLIENTS.
	  ○ One person from each group reads out their results.

Benefits:	Group Building, Communication, Rapport Builder, Imagination
Safety, Risks or Difficulties:	
Limits:	
Adaptations:	Can be adapted for use with Client / Patient groups by focusing on • HUMOUR YOURSELF and • HUMOURING OTHERS

Other considerations:	This exercise explores humour and play possibilities and gives imagination free reign. Working both individually and as a group increases range of possibilities. This activity is often noisy. It usually generates smiles.
Variations:	Pages can be displayed around the room

7 Next steps

Replenishing your humour quotient[1]

Once you have started on the path of introducing clown-plays into your practice, things tend to happen organically. There are several ways that you can help to improve your confidence, your timing and to expand your *Humour Quotient.*

Once begun – half done

- So I've started – what do I do now?
  - Repetition and practice are the keys to continuing success. Once you have tried and successfully used a couple of clown-plays there are several things you should consider.
    - If it ain't broke don't fix it
      - There is no harm in using the same play more than once with the same patient(s) / resident(s)
    - Slowly add to your repertoire
      - It is a good idea to be slowly and consistently adding to your repertoire of plays so that when you are told 'I've seen this, what else have you got', you have something new up your sleeve.
    - Work to improve your timing.
  - Maintain a journal
    - Keep notes on all the clown-plays you use and the context(s) in which you employ them
      - What worked well and what worked . . .not so much!
        - Any thoughts about why this was so.
        - How you think you can improve on what you did
      - Note reactions by patient(s) / resident(s)
  - Keep visual records
  - When and where appropriate take photographs / make videos of your work.
    - This will require gaining the necessary clearances and permissions to do so
    - In certain circumstances it may be possible to give patient(s) a Polaroid of the clown-play they just participated in.[2]
    - Works very well and can be a lot of fun with children and seniors

- Learning from your *mistakes – 'mistakes are your best teachers'*
    - When things do not go according to plan, take a moment to reflect on what went *wrong and what you can do next time to avoid the same problem occurring.*
    - As we have already mentioned it is important to
        - *Learn the rules so you know how to break them properly*
            - However sometimes this isn't enough and you must also know how best to apologise e.g. part of Clown-Doctor training is learning how to apologise in several different verbal and non-verbal ways with heart and humour.

Keeping yourself amused: ideas to humour yourself /your staff

It is important to be active in looking for ways to increase your repertoire of ideas and activities for use in your clown-play improve practice.

- Some simple things you can do include:
    - Go to
        - Conferences, that include workshops and talks on:
            - Arts and Health
            - Humour
            - Clown Skills
        - Workshops and / or courses[3] on:
            - Close-up magic
            - Clown Skills
            - Improv and / or comedy
            - Magic and / or toy stores
            - Bargain stores ($1, £1 etc.)
    - Watch:
        - Comedies
            - Even romantic comedies can produce some good material
        - Circus
        - Stand-up comics
        - Sitcoms
        - Political satire
        - Social media
            - YouTube
            - Facebook
            - Twitter
    - Build a resource library
        - Archive anything that you think may be useful in whatever format works for you whether this is:
            - A scrapbook
            - A file index
            - A digital site e.g. on an iPad or a smart phone or. . .

Figure 7.1 Smiles are everywhere

- Networking: Holding hands to share the load:
  - Try to find and share ideas with other like minded souls
    - Work together with one or two colleagues
    - Build a team or network
      - In your facility
      - In your local area
  - Start / Join a Listserve or Intranet
  - Try creative brainstorming.
    - Work in a groups to brainstorm possible ways to:
      - Humour yourself
      - Humour your staff and workplace environment
      - Humour your patients/residents/clients
  - Keep a record in your resource library

Our journey is done. We hope you, your colleagues and your patients, clients or residents have as much fun from using this book as we did writing it! For as you will see *Smiles Are Everywhere* and they are infectious!

Notes

1 *Humour Quotient*: If IQ (Intelligence Quotient) is considered one measure of a person's intelligence, then HQ is a measure of a person's capacity to respond positively to stressful events. People with high HQs are often more resilient to stress, and are often able to diffuse stressful situations by injecting smiles and laughter into them. (People like Robin Williams, Billy Connolly – both probably have a very high HQ.) If you wish you measure your own HQ see: http://www.greatleadershipbydan.com/2009/06/test-your-hq-humorquotient.html

2 Another option is to use a smart phone or digital camera and e-mail the picture to the patient/resident/client. However, there are several ethical issues with this in that a digital image may be stored and posted elsewhere, which is a *No-No!*

3 The authors both individually and together often run workshops and courses on the use of humour and play in healthcare settings. For more information go to: http://smilesareeverywhere.com/
Also see: The Association for Applied and Therapeutic Humor (AATH) website: http://www.aath.org The site includes information on resources, events, scholarships and more.

8 At-a-Glance Guide to clown-plays

		AUDIENCE		AGE				INTER-ACTION	
		Staff	Patients	Children	Adolescents	Adults	Seniors	Individual	Group
Name	**Name**								
1	This is my name & How I feel About	X	X	X	X	X	X		X
2	Where I Played As A Child	X	X		X	X	X		X
3	Meetings & Greetings	X	X		X	X	X		X
Verbal	**Verbal**								
4	Remembering Childhood Play	X	X		X	X	X		X
5	It Makes Me Happy When…	X	X		X	X	X	X	X
6	If you could have dinner with anyone	X	X			X	X	X	X
7	If I could be anywhere in the world	X	X	X	X	X	X	X	X
8	You'll never believe this but…	X	X		X	X	X	X	X
9	What am I holding?	X	X	X	X	X	X		X
10	What am I building?	X	X	X	X	X	X		X
11	Yes/No Story	X	X		X	X	X	X	X
Physical	**Physical**								
12	Chair Warm Up	X	X	X	X	X	X		X
13	Counting Fingers	X	X	X	X	X	X		X
14	Dancing Fingers	X	X	X	X	X	X		X
15	Mirror Face	X	X	X	X	X	X		X
16	Change Three Things	X	X	X	X	X	X		X
17	Boat Race	X	X		X	X			X
18	Walk Across the Room	X	X	X	X	X	X		X
19	Break My Balance	X	X		X	X			X
20	Are You There Mortiarty?	X	X		X	X			X
21	Dancing Cheek to Cheek	X	X		X	X			X
22	Mirror Work	X	X	X	X	X	X		X
23	Getting the Clap - Standing Ovation	X	X			X			X
24	These Are My Hands	X	X	X	X	X	X		X
25	Changing Chairs	X	X	X	X	X	X		X
26	Frau Holler Ist Krank	X	X	X	X	X	X		X
27	Love Heart Tennis	X	X		X	X	X		X
28	Jelly Belly (Ha Ha Ha)	X	X		X	X			X
29	Massage Train	X	X		X	X			X

LOCATION			DURATION			BENEFIT									
Bedside	Consult Room	Activity Room	Short	Medium	Long	Ice Breaker	Rapport	Memory	Communication	Stress Reduction	Diversionary	Group Building	Sensitivity	Physical	Imagination
X	X	X	X	X		X	X	X				X	X		
		X		X	X		X	X	X			X	X		
		X		X		X	X		X			X			X
		X		X			X	X	X	X			X		
X	X	X	X	X		X		X	X			X			X
X	X	X	X	X	?		X	?	X				X		X
X	X	X	X				X	X	X		X		X		X
X	X	X		X			X		X				X		X
		X	X	X			X		X				X		X
		X		X			X		X				X	X	
X	X	X	X	X			X		X				X		X
		X	X	X						X		X		X	
X	X	X	X			X	X		X	X		X			
		X	X				X		X				X	X	
		X	X			X			X	X			X		X
		X	X	X		X	X						X		X
		X	X				X		X	X		X	X	X	
		X	X	X			X		X			X		X	
		X	X				X		X				X	X	
		X	X			X			X	X			X	X	
		X	X				X		X	X			X	X	
		X	X	X	X		X		X				X	X	X
		X	X				X		X			X	X		
X	X	X	X	X			X	X	X			X	X		
		X	X	X	X		X		X	X				X	
		X	X	X				X	X			X		X	X
		X		X					X	X		X		X	
			X			X			X	X		X	X	X	
		X	X			X				X		X		X	

		AUDIENCE		AGE				INTERACTION	
		Staff	Patients	Children	Adolescents	Adults	Seniors	Individual	Group
Musical	**Musical**								
30	My Favourite Tunes	X	X		X	X	X		X
31	Song Circle	X	X		X	X	X		X
32	Juggling tunes	X	X		X	X			X
33	Stump The Chump	X	X	X	X	X	X		X
34	Cats and Dogs	X	X	X	X	X	X	X	X
Imaginative	**Imaginative**								
35	Look, Hold, Become	X	X	X	X	X	X		X
36	What are you Doing?	X	X	X	X	X	X		X
37	Sound Volley Ball	X	X		X	X			X
38	Imaginary Ball Toss	X	X		X	X			X
	Magical								
39	Stupid Magic	X	X	X	X	X	X	X	X
40	Squeaky Magic	X	X	X	X	X	X	X	X
41	Magic Newspaper	X	X		X	X			X
42	Tape Measure Telephone	X	X	X	X	X	X	X	X
43	Floating Cup		X	X				X	
44	Imp Bottle		X	X	X	X	X	X	
45	Magic Colouring Book		X	X				X	
46	D'Lite	X	X	X	X	X	X	X	X
47	Disappearing Silk	X	X	X	X	X	X	X	
48	Glove Balloon	X	X	X				X	
49	Magic Tongue Depressor		X	X				X	
50	Sponge Ball Magic	X	X	X	X	X	X	X	
Miscellaneous	**Miscellaneous**								
51	Finger Puppets		X	X	X	X	X	X	
52	Humour Cart	X	X	X	X	X	X		X
53	Humour Yourself	X				X			X

LOCATION			DURATION			BENEFIT									
Bedside	Consult Room	Activity Room	Short	Medium	Long	Ice Breaker	Rapport	Memory	Communication	Stress Reduction	Diversionary	Group Building	Sensitivity	Physical	Imagination
		X		X	X		X	X	X				X		
		X	X	X		X	X	X	X			X	X	X	
		X	X	X					X	X		X	X	X	
X	X	X	X	X		X	X	X	X	X	X	X	X	X	X
X	X	X	X			X	X	X	X	X		X		X	X
		X		X									X	X	X
		X		X	X	X	X		X	X		X			X
		X	X	X					X	X		X		X	X
		X		X		X			X	X		X		X	X
X	X	X	X				X		X		X				X
X	X	X	X				X		X		X				X
X	X	X		X		X				X		X			X
X	X	X	X						X		X				X
?	X		X				X		X		X				X
X	X	X	X			X	X		X		X				X
	X		X				X		X		X				X
X	X	X	X			X	X		X		X				X
X	X	X	X						X		X				X
	X		X			X	X				X			X	X
X	X	X	X			X	X		X		X			X	X
X	X	X	X			X	X		X		X				X
X	X		X				X		X		X				X
X	X	X	X			X	X		X						X
		X			X		X		X	X		X	X		X

References

Avedon, E. M. and Sutton-Smith, B. (1971). *The Study of Games*. R. E. Krieger Publishing Co., Huntington, New York.

Bailey, L. (2010a). Clown therapy program extends to homes' staff. *The Morning Report.* Retrieved from Ontario Long Term Care Association Website: http://www.oltca.com/axiom/DailyNews/2010/August/Aug27.html.

Bailey, L. (2010b). Clown therapy program impacting dementia residents. *The Morning Report.* Retrieved from Ontario Long Term Care Association Website: http://www.oltca.com/axiom/DailyNews/2010/June/June28.html.

Bailey, L. (2010c). Baycrest conference delivers does of information on humour and clown work. *The Morning Report.* Retrieved from Ontario Long Term Care Association Website: http://www.oltca.com/axiom/DailyNews/2010/March/March18.html.

Balick, M. J. and Lee, R. (2003). The role of laughter in traditional medicine and its relevance to the clinical setting: healing with Ha! *Alternative Therapies*, 9(4): 88–91.

Ballantine, B. (1982). *Clown Alley*. Little, Brown and Co., Boston, MA.

Ballard, C., O'Brien, J., James, I., Mynt, P., Lana, M., Potkins, D., Reichelt, K., Lee, L., Swann, A. and Fossey, J. (2001). Quality of life for people with dementia living in residential and nursing home care: the impact of performance on activities of daily living, behavioral and psychological symptoms, language skills. *International Psychogeriatrics*, 13(1): 93–106.

Battrick, C., Glasper, E. A., Prudhoe, G. and Weaver, K. (2007). Clown humour: the perceptions of doctors, nurses, parents and children. *Journal of Children's and Young People's Nursing*, 1(4): 174–179.

Bennett, M. and Lengacher, C. (2009). Humor and laughter may influence health: IV. Humor and immune function. *Evidence-based Complementary and Alternative Medicine*, 6: 159–164.

Bennett, M. and Lengacher, C. (2008). Humor and laughter may influence health: III. Laughter and health outcomes. *Evidence-based Complementary and Alternative Medicine*, 5: 37–40.

Bennett, M. and Lengacher, C. (2006b). Humor and laughter may influence health: II. Complementary therapies and humor in a clinical population. *Evidence-based Complementary and Alternative Medicine*, 3(2): 187–190.

Bennett, M. P. and Lengacher, C. A. (2006a). Humor and laughter may influence health. *Evidence-based Complementary and Alternative Medicine*, 3(1): 61–63

Berger, J. T., Coulehan, J. and Belling, C. (2004). Humor in the physician-patient encounter. *Archives of Internal Medicine*, 164: 825–830.

Berk, L. S., Tan, S. A., Napier, B. J. and Eby, W. C. 1989). Neuroendocrine and stress hormone change during mirthful laughter. *The American Journal of the Medical Sciences*, 298: 390–396.

Billington, S. (1984). *A Social History of the Fool*. Harvester Press, Brighton; St Martin's Press, New York.

Brodaty, H., Low, L-F., Spitzer, P., Bell, J-P., Chenoweth, L. and Fleming, R. Sydney Multisite Intervention of LaughterBosses and ElderClowns (SMILE) study, a randomized control trial of humour therapy in residential care. Three year grant (2009–12) from NHMRC (National Health and Medical Research Council, Australia).

Brown, S. (2009). *Play: How it Shapes the Brain, Opens the Imagination and Invigorates the Soul*. Avery, New York.

Buffum, M. D. and Brod, M. (1988). Humor and well-being in spouse caregivers of patients with Alzheimer's disease. *Applied Nursing Research*, 11(1): 12–18.

Callois, R. (1961). *Man, Play and Games*. Free Press of Glencoe, New York.

Cohen, D. (1987). *The Development of Play*. Croom Helm, Beckenham, Kent.

Cotlove, E. W. (1999). Letter re: research at Hippocrates hospital on Kos dated April 8th 1999.

Cousins, N. (1979). *Anatomy of an Illness*. Bantam, New York.

Dean, R. A. K. (2007). Expressing sensibilities: healing functions of humour in palliative care. In Warren, B. (Ed.) *Suffering the Slings and Arrows of Outrageous Fortune: International Perspectives on Stress, Laughter and Depression*. Rodopi, Amsterdam and New York, 191–206.

Dean, R. A. K. (1997). Humor and laughter in palliative care. *Journal of Palliative Care*, 13(1): 34–39.

Erasmus, D. (1946) [*1511 Reprint*]. *In Praise Of Folly*. Hendricks House, Farrar, Straus, New York.

Friedler, S., Glasser, S., Azani, L., Freedman, L .S., Raziel, A., Strassburger, D., Ron-El, R. and Lerner-Geva, L. (2011). The effect of medical clowning on pregnancy rates after in vitro fertilization and embryo transfer. *Fertility and Sterility*, 95(6): 2127–2130.

Fry, W. F. (1992). The physiologic effects of humor, mirth and laughter. *Journal of the American Medical Association*, 267: 1857–1858.

Fry, W. F. (1977). The respiratory components of mirthful laughter. *Journal of Biological Psychology*, 19: 39–50.

Fry, W. F. and Savin, M. (1988). Mirthful laughter and blood pressure. *Humor*, 1: 49–62.

Fry, W. F. and Stoft, P. E. (1971). Mirth and oxygen saturation levels on peripheral blood. *Psychotherapy Psychosomatic Medicine*, 19: 76–84.

Gelkopf, M. and Kreitler, S. (1996). Is humor only fun, an alternative cure or magic? The cognitive therapeutic potential of humor. *Journal of Cognitive Psychotherapy: An International Quarterly*, 10(4): 235–254.

Gibbons, J. C. (1899). *Douay-Rheims Bible*. Baronium Press, Glasgow.

Golan, G., Tighe, P., Dobija, N., Perel, A. and Keidan I. (2007). Clown as treatment for preoperative anxiety in children: a randomized controlled trial source. *Pediatric Anesthesia*, 19(3): 262–266.

Graneck-Catarivas, M., Goldstein-Ferber, S., Azuri, Y., Vinker, S. and Kahan, E. (2005). Use of humour in primary care: different perceptions among patients and physicians. *Postgraduate Medical Journal*, 81: 126–130.

Groos, K. (1896). *Die Spiele der Tiere* (Jena) [Translated by Baldwin, E. L. as *The Play of Animals* (1898) Appleton & Co., New York].

Hassed, C. (2001). How humour keeps you well. *Australian Family Physician*, 30(1): 25–28.

Hudak, D. A., Hudak, M. A. and DeGood, D. E. (1991). Effects of humorous stimuli and sense of humor on discomfort. *Psychological Reports*, 69: 779–786.

Huizinga, J. (1955). *Homo Ludens: A Study of the Play Element in Culture.* Beacon Press, Boston, MA.

Hyde, M. (2000). Clowning around. *Journal of the College of Physical and Surgeons of Columbia University*, 20: 22–24.

Jando, D. (2003). *Big Apple Circus – 25 years.* Big Apple Circus in association with Odyssey Guides, New York.

Killick, J. (2003). 'Funny and sad and friendly': a drama project in Scotland. *The Journal of Dementia Care*, 11(1): 24–26.

Kingnorth, S., Blain, S. and McKeever, P. (2010). Physiological and emotional responses of disabled children to Therapeutic Clowns: a pilot study. *Evidence-based Complementary and Alternative Medicine*, doi: 10.1093/ecam/neq008.

Koller, D. and Gryski, C. (2008). The life threatened child and the life enhancing clown: towards a model of therapeutic clowning. *Evidence-based Complementary and Alternative Medicine*, 5(1): 7–25.

Kontos, P. C. and Naglie, G. (2007). Expressions of personhood in Alzheimer's disease: an evaluation of research-based theatre as a pedagogical tool. *Qualitative Health Research*, 17(6): 799–811.

Levinson, W., Roter, D. L., Mullooly, J. P., Dull, V. T. and Frankel, R. M. (1997). Physician-patient communication: the relationship with malpractice claims among primary care physicians and surgeons. *Journal of the American Medical Association*, 277(7): 553–559.

Mahony, D. L, Burroughs, W. J. and Lippman, L. G. (2002). Perceived attributes of health-promoting laughter: a cross-generational comparison. *The Journal of Psychology*, 136(2): 171–181.

Mahony, D. L., Burroughs, W. J. and Hieatt, A. C. (2001). The effects of laughter on discomfort thresholds: does expectation become reality? *The Journal of General Psychology*, 128(2): 217–226.

Martin, R. A. (2004). Sense of humor and physical health: theoretical issues, recent findings, and future directions. *Humor: International Journal of Humor Research*, 17(1–2): 1–19.

Meincke, J. (2000). *ClownSprechstunde Lachen Ist Leben*. Verlag Hans Huber, Bern.

Miller, M., Mangano, C., Park, Y., Goel, R., Plotnick, G. D. and Vogel, R. A. (2006). Impact of cinematic viewing on endothelial function. *Heart*, 92: 261–262.

Mobbs, D., Greicius, M. D., Abdel-Azim, E., Menon, V. and Reiss, A. L. (2003). Humor modulates the mesolimbic reward centers. *Neuron*, 40(5): 1041–1048.

Morgan, A. and Jorm, A. (2008). Self-help interventions for depressive disorders and depressive symptoms: a systematic review. *Annals of General Psychiatry*, 7(1): 13.

O'Keefe, J. H., Poston, C. W. S., Haddock, C. K., Moe, R. M, and Harris, W. (2004). Psychosocial stress and cardiovascular disease: how to heal a broken heart. *Comprehensive Therapy*, 30(1): 37–43.

Oppenheimer, D., Simonds, C. and Hartmann, O. (1997). Clowning on children's wards. *The Lancet*, 350: 1838–1840.

Otto, B. K. (2001). *Fools are Everywhere: The Court Jester Around the World.* University of Chicago Press, Chicago, IL.

Penson, R. T., Partridge, R. A., Rudd, R., Seiden, M. V., Nelson, J. E., Chabner, B. A. and Lynch, T. J. (2005). Laughter: the best medicine? *Oncologist*, 10(8): 651–660.

Ptasznik, A. (2010). Not just clowning around. *Hospital News.* Retrieved from Hospital News Website: http://www.hospitalnews.com/modules/magazines/mag.asp?ID=3&IID=138&AID=1699.

Richman, J. (1995). The lifesaving function of humor with the depressed and suicidal elderly. *The Gerontologist*, 35: 271–273.

Rosner, F. (2002). Therapeutic efficacy of laughter in medicine. *Cancer Investigation*, 20(3): 434–436.

Schwebke, S. and Gryski, C. (2003). Gravity and levity – pain and play: the child and the clown in the pediatric health setting. In Klein, A. J. (Ed.) *Humor in Children's Lives: A Guidebook for Practice*. Praeger Publishers, Westport, CT pp. 49–68.

Simonds, C. and Warren, B. (2009). *Le Rire Médecin: Le Journal de Dr. Girafe*. Editions du Rire Médecin, Paris.

Simonds, C. and Warren, B. (2004). *The Clown Doctor Chronicles*, Rodopi, Amsterdam and New York.

Snyder, C. R. and Lopez, S. J. (2006). *Positive Psychology: The Science and Practical Explorations of Human Strengths*. Sage, London.

Solomon, J. C. (1996). Humor and aging well: a laughing matter or a matter of laughing? *American Behavioral Scientist*, 39(3): 249–271.

Spitzer, P. (2008). LaughterBoss: Introducing a new position in aged care. In Warren, B. (Ed.) *Using the Creative Arts in Healthcare and Therapy*. Routledge, London and New York.

Spitzer, P. (2006). Hospital clowns – modern-day court jesters at work. *The Lancet*, 368: 34–35.

Spitzer, P. (2001). The Clown Doctors. *Australian Family Physician*, 30(1): 12–16.

Sutorius, D. (1995). The transforming force of laughter, with focus on the laughing meditation. *Patient Educational Counselling*, 26: 367–371.

Sutton-Smith, B. (1979). *Play and Learning*. Gardner Press, New York.

Towsen, J. H. (1976). *Clowns*. Hawthorn, New York.

Vagnoli, L., Caprilli, S., Robiglio, A. and Messeri, A. (2005). Clown doctors as a treatment for preoperative anxiety in children: a randomized, prospective study. *Pediatrics*, 116(4): 563–567.

Van Blerkom, L. M. (1995). Clown-doctors: shaman healers of Western medicine. *Medical Anthropology Quarterly*, 9: 462–475.

Warren, B. (2011). *Drama Games (Revisited)*. Captus Press, North York, Ontario.

Warren, B. (2010). Foolish medicine: some connections between medieval Fools and Clown-Doctors. *Les Cahiers de l'idiotie*, 2(1): 145–164.

Warren, B. (2009b). Hi Jean!: How Clown-Doctors help facilitate infection control and positive health care practice. In Elliott, P. (Ed.) *Infection Control: A Practical Approach to Psychosocial Issues*. Radcliffe Publishing, Abingdon, Oxon pp. 149–158.

Warren, B. (2009a). Spreading sunshine . . . down memory lane: how clowns working in healthcare help promote recovery and rekindle memories. In Baum, N. T. (Ed.) *Come to Your Senses: Creating Supportive Environments to Nurture the Sensory Capital Within*. MukiBaum, Toronto pp. 37–44.

Warren, B. (2008b). Healing laughter: the role and benefits of Clown-Doctors working in hospitals and healthcare. In Warren, B. (Ed.) *Using the Creative Arts in Healthcare and Therapy*. Routledge, London and New York p. 228.

Warren, B. (2008a). The fools are come hither. *Research in Drama in Education*, 13(3): 365–369.

Warren, B. (Ed) (2006). *Suffering the Slings and Arrows of Outrageous Fortune: International Perspectives on Stress, Laughter and Depression*. Rodopi, Amsterdam and New York.

Warren, B. (2004). Bring me sunshine: the effects of Clown-Doctors on the mood and attitudes of health care staff. In Twohig, P. and Kalitzkus, V. (Eds.) *Interdisciplinary Perspectives on Health Illness and Disease.* Rodopi, Amsterdam and New York pp. 83–96.

Warren, B. (2003). Treating wellness: how clown-doctors help to humanise healthcare and promote good health. In Twohig, P. and Kalitzkus, V. (Eds.) *Making Sense of Health, Illness and Disease.* Rodopi, Amsterdam and New York pp. 201–216.

Warren, B. (2002). Fools for health: introducing clown-doctors to Windsor hospitals. In B. Warren (Ed.) *Creating a Theatre in Your Classroom and Community*. Captus University Publications, North York, Ontario pp. 225–246.

Warren, B. (2001). What do clown doctors know and how do they learn to do what they do? *NALL Working Paper #43-2001.*

Warren, B. and Spitzer, P. (2011). Laugh to longevity: the work of elder-clowns with seniors in residential care facilities. *The Lancet*, 378: 562–563.

Weaver, K., Prudhoe, G., Battrick, C. and Glasper, E. A. (2007). Sick children's perceptions of clown doctor humor. *Journal of Children's and Young People's Nursing*, 1(8): 359–365.

Weinstein, M. and Goodman, J. (1980). *Everybody's Guide to Noncompetitive Play: Playfair.* Impact, Atascadero, CA.

Weisenberg, M., Tepper, I. and Schwarzwald, J. (1995). Humor as a cognitive technique for increasing pain tolerance. *Pain*, 63(2): 207–212.

Welsford, E. (1968) [1935 Reprint]. *The Fool: His Social and Literary History*. Faber and Faber, London.

Westburg, N. (2003). Hope, laughter, and humor in residents and staff at an assisted living facility. *Journal of Mental Health Counseling*, 25(1): 16–32.

Willeford, W (1969). *The Fool and His Scepter.* Northwestern University Press, Evanston, IL.

Williams, H. (1986). Humor and healing: Therapeutic effects in geriatrics. *Gerontion* 1(3): 14–17.

Winnicott, D. W. (1971). *Playing and Reality*. Tavistock, London.

Author Index

Subject Index